LIFTING DEPRESSION

The Chromium Connection

Malcolm Noell McLeod, M.D.

Basic Health
PUBLICATIONS, INC.

The information contained in this book is based upon the research and personal and professional experiences of the author. It is not intended as a substitute for consulting with your physician or other healthcare provider. Any attempt to diagnose and treat an illness should be done under the direction of a healthcare professional.

The publisher does not advocate the use of any particular healthcare protocol but believes the information in this book should be available to the public. The publisher and author are not responsible for any adverse effects or consequences resulting from the use of the suggestions, preparations, or procedures discussed in this book. Should the reader have any questions concerning the appropriateness of any procedures or preparation mentioned, the author and the publisher strongly suggest consulting a professional healthcare advisor.

Basic Health Publications, Inc.
28812 Top of the World Drive
Laguna Beach, CA 92651
949-715-7327

Library of Congress Cataloging-in-Publication Data

McLeod, Malcolm Noell, 1938–
    Lifting depression : the chromium connection / by Malcolm Noell McLeod.
    p. cm.
    Includes bibliographical references and index.
    ISBN-13: 978-1-59120-164-9
    ISBN-10: 1-59120-164-0
    1. Depression, Mental—Alternative treatment. 2. Chromium—Therapeutic use.
I. Title.
RC537.M3975   2005
616.85'27061—dc22
                                                          2005015025

Editor: Cheryl Hirsch
Typesetting/Book design: Theresa Wiscovitch
Cover design: Mike Stromberg

Printed in the United States of America

10   9   8   7   6   5   4   3   2   1

Contents

To the Reader, vii
Foreword, ix
Acknowledgments, xi

PART ONE

Coping with Depression

1. Life Is a Burden, 3
2. Recognizing a Disorder, 8
3. Looking for Causes, 13
4. Formulating a Treatment Plan, 19
5. Taking the Back Roads, 23
6. The Long Way Home, 26
7. Murder of the Senses, 31

PART TWO

Finding One of Nature's Secrets

8. A Ray of Light, 37
9. A Miracle in Nature, 42
10. Needle in a Haystack, 47
11. Land Ahoy, 52
12. Elizabeth: A Careful Observer, 61
13. Do No Harm, 66
14. Sara: Lost and Wounded, 74
15. Giving Sorrow Words, 81

PART THREE

From Observation to Explanation

16. A Prepared Mind, 89
17. A Lock and a Key, 93
18. Sadness and Long Sorrow, 99

PART FOUR

A Beautiful New Vista

19. An Undergraduate in Experience, 109
20. Joseph: Insulin Resistance Syndrome, 123
21. The Sky Turns Clear and Blue, 133
22. Help from Experts, 140
23. Proof, 146

PART FIVE

There, and Back Again

24. A Grateful Psychiatrist, 153
25. Where It All Began, 162
26. Our Paths Crossed for a Moment, 166
27. Putting It All Together, 173

Appendices, 181
Glossary, 191
Internet Resources, 193
References, 197
Index, 207

In memory of
Dr. Walter Mertz

To wrest from nature the secrets that have perplexed philosophers in all ages, to track to their sources the causes of diseases, to correlate the vast stores of knowledge, that they may be quickly available for the prevention and cure of disease—these are our ambitions.

—SIR WILLIAM OSLER (1849–1919)
early advocate of holistic medicine and first professor of medicine at Johns Hopkins Hospital

To the Reader

If you have opened this book, chances are that you feel depressed, or know someone who is. Depression is a treatable illness.

In addition to feeling depressed, do you have any of the following symptoms:

☐ Do you crave sweets or starchy carbohydrates and have a tendency to overeat?

☐ Do you feel hungry or shaky an hour or two after eating carbohydrates—for example, after eating pancakes with maple syrup or a rich dessert?

☐ Are you often excessively sleepy for no known reason?

☐ Do your arms and legs feel heavy, as if they are made of lead?

☐ Are your feelings easily hurt by others?

If you answered "yes" to one or more of these questions, it is quite likely that you are suffering from the type of depression known as atypical depression.

"Atypical" is a misnomer, as it implies that this type of depression is rare. It is not. In fact, it is the most common type of depression. Over half of the depressed patients I see in my psychiatric practice are suffering from atypical depression. There is a class of medications that helps atypical depression, but these antidepressants are dangerous and seldom prescribed. Until now there has been no specific treatment for atypical depression that is both safe and free of side effects.

In these pages, I will tell you about my discovery of a new and natural treatment for atypical depression, how I discovered it, and what you can do to help yourself.

Foreword

Shortly after arriving into the United States from England in 1972, it was my good fortune to meet Dr. Malcolm McLeod. We immediately recognized our common desire to find better and safer treatments for depression, and began a most productive collaboration, which continued over the next few years. I was therefore delighted when, after a hiatus of about two decades, Dr. McLeod called to tell of his most exciting discoveries with chromium, which quickly stimulated my interest, and echoed back to the days of our successful collaboration in the 1970s.

The story told by Dr. McLeod in *Lifting Depression: The Chromium Connection* is rare and important. Rare, because clinical practice doesn't easily allow for the development and testing of hypotheses; to do so is an arduous undertaking, and calls for great dedication and focus. It is important because depression remains one of the world's biggest health problems and cause of disability, as has been demonstrated by the World Bank/World Health Organization Global Project.

The need for safe, effective, and inexpensive treatments is paramount, and Dr. McLeod's discoveries may well lead to the introduction of an important new treatment for depression. I am therefore honored for the opportunity to write this introduction.

I reviewed many of Dr. McLeod's extensive notes and was impressed by his careful and impeccably documented observations. I interviewed his patients, some of whom reported that chromium had increased the efficacy of their antidepressant medications, while others reported that chromium picolinate *alone* lifted their depression.

There was no doubt, in my mind, that this deserved the most serious consideration. Given the limitations of our current standard treatments for depression, the potential for chromium as a new and well-tolerated treatment seemed exceptionally strong. As a result, I decided to conduct a clinical trial based on the highest scientific standards, that is, placebo-controlled and double-blinded. The study was conducted at the Duke University Medical Center, and the results were surprisingly positive.

When the code was broken and I learned who had been taking chromium picolinate, I was very gratified to learn that chromium had proved to be more effective than the placebo. I called Dr. McLeod and told him of our striking results and remember saying to him, "A researcher waits an entire lifetime for a moment such as this."

In summary, Dr. McLeod's book, *Lifting Depression: The Chromium Connection,* is not a typical self-help book, but is one that truly takes us through a fascinating journey shared by a psychiatrist and his patients, a journey that suggests an intriguing connection between depression, insulin resistance, and the role of chromium. This is unquestionably an uplifting, powerful story that will deliver hope and help to millions of people.

—Jonathan R.T. Davidson, M.D.
Professor of Psychiatry
Duke University Medical Center, Durham, North Carolina

Acknowledgments

I greatly admire and appreciate the patients described in this book. They were (and still are) my best teachers. I shall always be indebted to them and they know that. Each of them has read and approved his or her case history for publication. Indeed, they have encouraged me to reveal their stories, hoping that others will be helped as much as they have by adding chromium picolinate to their treatment regimen for depression. Although I have changed all identifying details to preserve their confidentiality, I have tried to faithfully report their inner beauty and noble struggles.

I am fortunate to have made friends with world-class physician/scientists who affirmed and encouraged my research. Robert N. Golden, M.D., vice dean of the University of North Carolina School (UNC) of Medicine, professor and chair of psychiatry at UNC, and a National Institute of Mental Health-educated psychiatric researcher took time from his busy schedule to listen to me. We spoke face to face, over the phone, and exchanged literally thousands of e-mail messages as he guided me in clinical research. Although initially skeptical, as was I, he was always open-minded and willing to let the evidence speak. He and members of his staff interviewed patients who had responded to chromium; they made valuable suggestions; and we wrote two scientific articles, one describing the use of chromium to enhance the efficacy of antidepressant medications, and the second describing the use of chromium alone in the treatment of depression.

James O. McNamara, M.D., who is the Carl R. Deane professor of neuroscience and chair of the Department of Neurobiology at Duke University Medical Center, provided the unique perspective of an experienced neurological (as opposed to psychiatric) researcher, providing insights as to how chromium might work on a molecular level to relieve depression.

Dr. McNamara was so enthusiastic and always welcomed reports of the latest bit of new information. He also had great practical advice: he advised me to submit patent applications covering my discoveries. Without patent coverage I would have been unable to interest a corporation in extending my research.

My constant friend, James R. Weiss, M.D., a psychiatrist and psychoanalyst in private practice in the Chapel Hill-Durham area, patiently listened to me describe one patient after another who had responded to chromium and those who had not. I was concerned I might be boring him with my constant preoccupation with my research, and occasionally would force myself to turn to another topic, only to have Dr. Weiss, once again, inquire about the latest chromium developments. Dr. Weiss had a broad perspective and, thus, was often able to articulate my findings better than I; he also helped me organize my thoughts. As Thoreau said: "It takes two to tell the truth: one to speak it and one to listen."

I was also grateful when Jonathan R.T. Davidson, M.D., entered the picture. A professor of psychiatry at Duke University Medical Center and a world-acclaimed psychiatric investigator, Dr. Davidson eagerly agreed to conduct the first double-blinded, placebo-controlled, clinical trial on the use of chromium in the treatment of depressed people who had excessive appetite and fatigue. I will always remember the day Dr. Davidson called to tell me that the chromium-treatment-of-depression study had been completed and the data analyzed. In a voice filled with excitement, he exclaimed, "The results of the study strongly support your hypothesis that chromium helps atypical depression."

I thank Adam Vardaman and other staff members of the Health Sciences Library at the University of North Carolina. They helped me find hundreds of articles, some of them over 100 years old and in obscure journals.

I appreciate the help of developmental editors Sara Rogers Miller and Elizabeth Lyon who helped me get the manuscript in shape to present to publishers.

It was my good fortune to meet publisher Norman Goldfind. After talking with him for a short while about my discovery, I realized he was a warm person and I wanted him to publish my book. I asked him to do so and was delighted to find he was willing and eager.

I am indebted to my last editor, Cheryl Hirsch, whose gentle encouragement enabled me to stop fretting, stop revising, stop holding on to the manuscript, and with some sadness, say goodbye to it.

I am especially grateful for the forbearance of my family, as I spent many weekends and evenings in the library over several years. Their confidence in me is, and always has been, a source of great inspiration. I hope I have given them as much as they have given me.

PART ONE

Coping with Depression

CHAPTER 1

Life Is a Burden

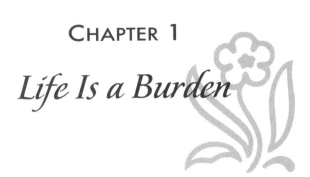

Life is a burden to me.
—GEORGE

This story begins in the early 1990s. It was one of those clear, warm, March days in North Carolina that heralds the imminent birth of a beautiful spring, so generous in fragrance and color. I was looking out my office window, watching a few clouds calmly drifting across an otherwise clear blue sky, when I heard my waiting room door open, announcing the arrival of my new patient, George.

I went out to introduce myself. Slowly, George stood up. He glowered at me as we shook hands. I was unable to "read" his facial expression well enough to tell whether he was sad or angry, but he was unmistakably distressed.

George Begins His Story

I invited George into my office. After we were seated, I asked him why he had asked to see me, a psychiatrist.

George answered, "I don't want to admit it, but I feel so down, so blue, so discouraged and depressed. And I'm hungry and tired almost all the time. I crave sweets, and pasta and bread. I overeat until I'm physically uncomfortable, and I feel guilty about that. Since I'm on the heavy side, I have to exercise a lot to control my weight, but now I'm so tired I have to force myself to put one foot in front of the other. My arms—and especially my legs—feel heavy, almost like I'm walking in molasses. I've lost my ability to enjoy life. Take today for example, I can see how beautiful it is, but I don't feel the beauty. Life is a burden to me."

3

I asked him, "How old are you, and how long have you felt this way?"

George answered, "I'm fifty years old, and I've felt this way since I was in my twenties. I feel worse sometimes more than others, but traces of depression are always there. It's such a contrast to the way I felt when I was young. Back then I had a lot of enthusiasm."

By this time it was clear to me that George was not simply *feeling* depressed. He *was* depressed. All of us feel depressed or sad occasionally, when for example we are disappointed in someone or after we read a sad book, or after a loved pet dies. But these feelings last only a few days or weeks, and they do not interfere with how our body works.

Being depressed, on the other hand, is a medical disorder, an illness that affects our basic body functions. There are several illnesses that we call depression, and they show up in different ways. For example, our appetite is excessive and we eat too much, or we don't have an appetite and we don't eat enough. We lose weight or we gain weight. We lack energy and feel exhausted or we are agitated. We don't sleep well or we can't stay awake. We are so depressed that we don't react to what others say or do, or we overreact to the slightest criticism. Our mind races, or our ability to think and concentrate is slowed down. We have suffered from depression since childhood or we feel fine until depression begins in our mid-thirties or later.

In George's case, his appetite was excessive, he felt exhausted for no obvious reason, and his depression began in his twenties. This type of depression is known in medical parlance as "atypical depression." That's an unfortunate name, as it implies that atypical depression is rare, when in fact it is the most common type of depression I have seen in my thirty years of outpatient practice.

I needed to ask George some questions to find out if he had more symptoms of atypical depression, so I asked, "When positive events happen in your personal life or at work, does your mood lift?"

He answered, "My depressed mood used to lift when something good would happen to me. I'd be really cheerful for awhile, but within a few days gloom would descend on me again. As I've gotten older, it's almost like my mood is frozen. I don't have the up periods anymore. Now my mood seldom lifts when something good happens."

I asked George, "Are you irritable or overly sensitive in your interactions with people?"

He thought for a moment and then said, "That's been somewhat of a problem. When my depression first started, I'd snap at people when I shouldn't. As the years have gone by, my irritability is less, but I've become too touchy, too 'thin skinned.' I'll even feel like crying over the smallest things, like if someone doesn't say 'Good morning' just right. That's a bit of an exaggeration. A better example is that I tear up too easily, like when I say the blessing before meals or when I hear an old hymn at church."

I needed to find out if he felt this way at any particular time of the day, so I asked, "Do you feel worse in the morning or in the afternoon, or can you notice any difference?"

George nodded and said, "I feel worse later in the day. It's worse around 5:00 P.M. or so."

I continued gathering diagnostic information and asked, "You mentioned you toss and turn at night. Do you now—or have you ever—had a problem with sleeping too much?"

George answered, "I've never had a problem with sleeping too much. As I've gotten older, I have some trouble falling asleep, but the main problem is that my sleep is not restful. Because I don't sleep well during the night, I often feel sluggish or dull during the day, and my concentration is not what I'd like it to be."

George's Background

I said to George, "As important as it is to understand your symptoms and make a correct diagnosis, I want to know you as a person and about your background. Where did you grow up? What were your early years like?"

He answered, "As I said, I'm fifty years old. I come from a poor family. I mean really poor. There were times when we worried about having a roof over our heads and if we'd have food on the table. Dad was a sweet man and proud of me when he was sober, but unfortunately he was a full-blown alcoholic. He went on binges that lasted weeks at a time. He lost jobs due to his drinking. He even lost a union job, and that's hard to do. Mom probably was an alcoholic too, as she drank a lot. She was unhappy—depressed I guess you'd say—and I could never please her.

"I started working at an early age to help support my younger brothers and sisters. I shoveled snow off the neighbors' driveways to make money, and I loved it. Up north everybody hates snow, but when I saw the first flake fall, it made me happy because I knew I'd have another job soon. I also delivered papers before school, and at night I worked in a grocery store bagging groceries and stocking shelves. I enjoyed working back then.

"I'm the only one in my family who ever went to college. The only way I was able to go to college is because I received a football scholarship. My brothers and sisters started working in the factories after they graduated from high school. They spend a lot of time in bars drinking and watching sporting events."

I asked him if he had ever sought treatment for depression.

He took a deep breath and sighed, "Over the years, I have gone to several psychotherapists for short periods of time. I've seen a few marriage counselors also, and from time to time have talked with my minister. Most of them were good people. By "good" I mean they had good intentions, and they helped me cope with how I was feeling at the time, but they never got to the bottom of my problem, to why I was feeling so bad. I've also been to Overeaters Anonymous and Adult Children of Alcoholics."

I continued to seek a full understanding of his background and asked, "Have you ever tried an antidepressant medication?"

George replied, "No. A psychiatrist, who occasionally breezed in and out of one of the groups I had attended, suggested I take an antidepressant, but I didn't follow his advice. I felt he was offering me a pill without knowing me at all, or at least certainly not in-depth. Plus, I've heard they have bad side effects and I don't want that."

"Have you tried any other treatments for your depression?" I asked.

He answered, "You seem conservative to me, and I'm afraid you'll think I'm ridiculous, but over the past two decades, I've read every self-help book known to man. I've tried the sugar buster's diet. Whenever I eat sugar or too much bread and pasta, I feel better for awhile, but in an hour or two I'm even hungrier than I was before. It's a vicious cycle. When I cut back on carbs and eat more protein and some fat, I feel somewhat better. I take omega-3 fatty acids. I take vitamins and minerals daily. Do you think I'm spinning my wheels?"

"No," I replied. "And you're right. I am conservative. I only recommend treatments that have been proven to be effective and safe. But, as the years have gone by, I have realized what a complex disorder depression is. There are many causes of depression, and many treatments. What you're doing sounds reasonable to me."

Close of First Session

I could almost feel the weight of George's depression from what he said, and how he said it.

As our first session was drawing to a close, I said to him, "I've learned a little about you as a person and a few facts about the type of depression that is troubling you. I need to learn a lot more before making a treatment recommendation. But first, I need to make certain you are safe. "Your comment, 'Life is a burden to me,' concerns me that you might be suicidal. Do you have thoughts of ending your life, or do you have a plan to take your life?"

George answered, "I want to die. I would like to. I'm so tired. But I can't take my life. I'd let too many people down—my family, friends, and the employees of my company. They depend on me. I just couldn't."

Then, after hesitating a moment, he added, "My company would not survive without me. If I died, it would fold, and my employees would be left high and dry, without any means of support. I know what that's like. I just couldn't do that to them, but—just in case—I've applied for a life-insurance policy that would give each of my employees a year's salary if I died."

"I appreciate your candor. That's so important in our work," I told him. "I want you to tell me when you feel suicidal, but I want to prevent any suicide attempt. Are you able to make a contract with me that you won't try to take your life, and that if such urges became irresistible, you will call me?" George promised he would.

I wanted to meet with George again as soon as possible and therefore proposed we meet early the next morning. He agreed and our first session ended.

As he walked out of my office, I found myself wondering, why is such a fine person—so concerned about the welfare of others—unable to extend that kindness to himself? I hoped he would keep his next appointment and I would be able to learn more about him and lessen his suffering.

CHAPTER 2

Recognizing a Disorder: Identifying Atypical Depression

To learn how to treat disease, one must learn how to recognize it.
—JEAN MARTIN CHARCOT (1825–1893), *founder of modern neurology*

Before my next meeting with George, I was thinking about him and his difficulties.

Symptoms of Atypical Depression

It became obvious to me that George was suffering from the type of depression known as atypical depression, which may affect as many as 30 million Americans. A person with this type of depression not only feels down or blue, but he or she also has at least one or more of the following symptoms:

- **Early age of onset, before age thirty.** Atypical depression often begins gradually, sometimes as early as the teenage years, and it may last a lifetime if untreated.[1–2] This early age of onset is in contrast to the type of depression known as "melancholic depression," which usually occurs in persons in their thirties or forties and begins quite rapidly over a few days or weeks. The onset and course of atypical depression is to melancholic depression as a long, gray winter is to a summer thunderstorm. George's depression began when he was in his twenties. It came about gradually. Therefore, he had endured it for most of his adult life.

- **Excessive hunger or weight gain when depressed.** One of the main symptoms of atypical depression is excessive appetite, which often results in weight gain. This is one of the most consistent symptoms that identifies atypical depression.[3] George was excessively hungry, and he had a tendency to put on weight. He was especially fond of sweets. This symptom was quite severe with George, as he had been struggling with excessive hunger and resultant weight gain for most of his adult life.

- **Unexplained exhaustion.** Many people with atypical depression say that they feel exhausted for no obvious reason.[4] Often they say their arms and legs feel heavy and weighted down, as if made of lead. This symptom troubled George considerably. As he described it, "I often feel like I'm walking in molasses."

- **Mood reactivity.** The depressed mood of people with atypical depression can lift in response to favorable events, but depression soon returns. Not all patients with atypical depression have this characteristic. This symptom may apply more to women than men.[5] George definitely exhibited this symptom in the early years of his life. When he was a young man, his mood would lift in response to positive events, such as seeing an enjoyable movie or having a success at work. However, as the months of his depression stretched into years, eventually his depressed mood became almost "fixed," and hardly ever lifted when something favorable happened.

- **Sensitivity to any perceived criticism or rejection.** Many people with atypical depression will overreact to the slightest real or perceived criticism with anger or anxiety. Some people with atypical depression have an intense form of anxiety around people, an anxiety described as social phobia.[6–7] Oftentimes others in close association with the person will comment, "Why did you get so upset about that? I can't see why something like that would bother you so much." Being excessively sensitive often causes the person with atypical depression to avoid social encounters with people, as well as makes others feel uncomfortable around them.[8] This anxiety about whether one is valued, which leads to heightened sensitivity, can begin early—even as early as in elementary school. George was perhaps somewhat more sensitive than most to being criticized, but his sensitivity to rejection was not severe.

- **Excessive sleeping.** Many people with atypical depression sleep too much.[9] George never had this problem. The amount of sleep he did get, however, was not restful.

This "mix" of symptoms in atypical depression varies from person to person, just as symptoms of flu vary. Some people who contract the flu virus have fever and headache, while other people with the same virus have fever and upset stomach or muscle aches. In George's case, he had three of the main symptoms of atypical depression: early age of onset, excessive hunger, and unexplained exhaustion. George was not troubled at this time by the other three symptoms. Earlier in his life, his mood lifted in response to favorable events, but this symptom gradually disappeared, as he grew older in that his depressed mood remained constant. He was not especially sensitive to criticism and he did not have the symptom of excessive sleepiness.

How Typical Is Atypical Depression?

The term "atypical depression" is misleading, as it implies that this disorder is rare. It is not. Many recent studies have documented that atypical depression is a distinct subtype of depression that has its own set of symptoms. The concept of atypical depression is fairly recent. Unfortunately, to this very day, the disorder is often overlooked by many mental health professionals.

According to the results of a study published in 1998, atypical depression is the most common type of depression seen in outpatient settings. Psychiatrist Andrew A. Nierenberg, M.D., of the Depression Clinical and Research Program of Massachusetts General Hospital in Boston, and his colleagues, interviewed 396 persons who came to the hospital's outpatient psychiatric clinic seeking relief from depression.[10] Of this group, 166—a whopping 42 percent—had atypical depression. By contrast only 12 percent had the next most frequent type of depression, known as typical or melancholic depression. If atypical depression is so common, why is it called "atypical"?

The first type of depression to be recognized was the type associated with weight loss, loss of appetite, severe insomnia, self-loathing, and suicidal thoughts. This type is known as melancholic depression. It has been known and described since the time of Hippocrates. For many years melancholia was thought to be the only type of depression. The differences from person to person were explained as variations in severity of the same illness.

However, in the 1950s, two psychiatrists at the St. Thomas's Hospital in London, Drs. E.D. West and P.J. Dally, recognized that a biologically different type of depression was the "opposite" of melancholia in that the person has an increase in appetite, weight gain, and excessive sleepiness. To distinguish this type of depression from melancholia, they coined the term "atypical" depression. This term, misleading as it is, has remained in use since that time.

Discovering a Treatment for Atypical Depression

In the 1950s a medication called iproniazid was developed for the treatment of tuberculosis.[11] Before the discovery of iproniazid, there was no medical treatment for this feared, highly contagious, and often-fatal disease. To prevent its spread, the only treatment available was to move tubercular patients away from family, friends, and loved ones and quarantine them into special hospitals called sanatoriums. Understandably, many of the patients became depressed.

Many years ago, as a medical student, I made rounds and examined patients with tuberculosis at Gravely Sanatorium in Chapel Hill, North Carolina. The atmosphere was heavy with fear and despair. Before examining the patients, we had to don a mask, gown, and gloves. As I was listening to their chests with a stethoscope, I wondered what they were feeling emotionally. I looked into their eyes and thought I saw resignation and fear. It is difficult for us to imagine today how painful that isolation must have been.

When iproniazid was being given to patients with tuberculosis and its efficacy was being evaluated, to the great surprise of the physicians, the patients' depression lifted rapidly and they felt more energetic as well. This lead was pursued by psychiatrists and researchers who found that iproniazid was indeed helpful, especially in patients with atypical depression. This was one of the major advances in medicine in the twentieth century.

It was correctly assumed that iproniazid slowed down the effect of something called monoamine oxide enzyme in the brain, and it was therefore called a monoamine oxidase inhibitor (MAOI). Monoamine oxide is an enzyme, which breaks down the "feel good chemicals" serotonin and norepinephrine in the brain. By "inhibiting" this breakdown and therefore allowing more of these chemicals to remain in the brain longer, iproniazid caused a person's depressed mood to lift.

Both psychiatrists and depressed patients alike were elated when they learned about the antidepressant effects of iproniazid. Thousands of prescriptions for iproniazid were written for persons suffering from depression. Several scientific studies confirmed iproniazid's antidepressant properties.

Danger of MAOIs

The high hopes that a treatment for atypical depression had been found were dashed when it became quickly apparent that iproniazid was associated with the death of several patients due to liver failure. As a result, iproniazid was withdrawn.

During the 1960s, newer MAOIs were developed that were not toxic to the liver. They were highly effective in treating atypical depression. However, these newer MAOIs, while not damaging to the liver, were potentially highly toxic in another way. When someone who is taking an MAOI eats foods containing the amino acid derivative tyramine, his or her blood pressure almost immediately spikes to a dangerous level, which often causes a fatal stroke. A wide range of foods contain tyramine. Some of these include aged cheeses, tenderized meat, preserved fish, chicken livers, beef liver, avocados, broad beans, red wine, sour cream, yogurt, game meats, bananas, figs, and soy sauce. It was also found that some over-the-counter cold medications, taken with a MAOI, can also cause death due to the sudden violent increase in blood pressure.

Although MAOIs are the most effective antidepressant medication for atypical depression, almost no psychiatrists prescribe them and most patients understandably refuse to take them after being informed about their potentially dangerous side effects. This means that the millions of people with atypical depression are not receiving adequate treatment.

Looking Forward to the Next Meeting with George

I was aware that George had atypical depression from his description of his symptoms, but I did not know what was causing his depression. I wanted to focus our next meeting on a search for possible clues.

Even though I did not know of an effective, safe, specific medical treatment for atypical depression, I was aware of some general measures that are often helpful, including psychotherapy, a healthy diet, and exercise.

But what neither of us could have anticipated was the discovery of an ordinary substance, an essential nutrient found in trace amounts in the human body that would be amazingly effective and specific in relieving atypical depression with *no* toxicity and *no* side effects.

The story of that discovery is revealed in the following pages.

CHAPTER 3

Looking for Causes

> *One cannot possibly practice good medicine and not*
> *understand the fundamentals underlying therapy.*
> —FULLER ALBRIGHT (1900–1969), *American physician and endocrinologist*

While I was waiting for George to come for his second session, I reminded myself that, although I was able to *describe* his cluster of symptoms as characteristic of atypical depression, I did not know the underlying *cause* of his depression. Simply giving a name to a cluster of symptoms is just the first step. My next task was trying to find out *why* George was depressed.

Causes of Typical and Atypical Depression

There are many psychological and nonpsychological causes of all types of depression. To rule out the nonpsychological or medical causes, a depressed person should have a complete medical examination by his or her family doctor.

One physiological cause of depression is an underlying medical condition. General medical disorders are notorious for masquerading as depression. For instance, one of my patients had Cushing's syndrome—a disorder that causes too much of the stress hormone cortisol to be present in the body. This condition causes the person to gain weight (especially around the abdomen), have high blood pressure, and be susceptible to infections. When Cushing's syndrome is treated, the patient's depression lifts right away.

Several of my patients had depression that was traced to hypothyroidism, a condition caused when a person has too little thyroid hormone, and therefore feels not only depressed, but also tired and sluggish much of the time. Administration of thyroid hormone relieves depression.

Numerous other medical conditions can also cause depression, such as vitamin B_{12} deficiency, diabetes, multiple sclerosis, hepatitis, and certain viral infections of the brain (encephalitis). A thorough medical examination should reveal any underlying medical condition that may be contributing to depression.

Another physiological cause of depression is taking prescription medications. Some of these medications include steroids, antihypertensives, birth control pills, and medication for Parkinson's disease, which is itself a medical condition that is often an underlying cause of depression. Other physiological causes can be a withdrawal from "street" drugs such as amphetamines and cocaine. Excessive alcohol consumption can be another cause of depression as well.

George Returns

The sound of the waiting room door opening took me out of my reverie. I was relieved that George had returned for his second visit. I was looking forward to beginning the search for the cause of his depression, which he had endured for so many years.

I went out to the waiting room to invite him in. He had the same countenance as he did during our first meeting—a grim facial expression with a furrowed brow. He walked into my office slowly, despondently, and stoop-shouldered. After he sat down, George asked if I usually see people so early in the morning. I told him I was not inconvenienced and that I wanted to see him as soon as possible as it was obvious how much he was suffering.

Looking for Causes of George's Depression

I told George that I wanted to find out more about him as a person and about his difficulties. The best way to begin, I suggested, was to try to find out what was causing his depression. He readily agreed.

Physical or Medical Conditions

I said to George, "I'd like to begin by ruling out any physical or medical cause of your depression. Is it OK with you if we start there?"

He nodded and said, "That sounds reasonable to me. I've thought all along that something is wrong with my body and whatever it is, it's causing my depression."

I asked George, "Why have you thought that?"

He answered, "Because it's not normal to feel hungry and tired most of the time. I eat so much I get physically uncomfortable. I have trouble concentrating and my muscles ache. I couldn't think of any good reason why I was depressed. Nothing bad has happened to me that would explain it. Just the reverse. My life is going well, yet I'm down. That's why I went to my family doctor last month and told him I thought there was something wrong with my body that was causing my depression."

"Please tell me in as much detail as possible about the visit with him and what the doctor said," I told him.

George nodded his head. "He said he thought I might have diabetes. He wanted to do a blood test for it."

"Did he tell you why he thought that?" I asked.

"Yes, because I'm overweight, I crave sweets, and several members of my mother's family had diabetes—the adult type—and they were overweight too. He called me a few days later and said all the blood tests were normal, including my blood sugar, and that I didn't have diabetes. He said, though, that he thought I might have what he called pre-diabetes and I might become diabetic later, especially if I didn't take the weight off. But he couldn't find anything wrong. That's why he referred me to you."

George assured me that his family physician had conducted a thorough physical examination and done extensive laboratory tests, and had not found any underlying medical condition.

I said to George, "Prescription medications, street drugs, and excessive consumption of alcohol can cause depression. Do any of these causes seem a likely cause of your depression?"

George indicated that he drank very little alcohol, as he was afraid of becoming alcoholic like his parents. He said that he did not take any prescription medications or street drugs, and that the only pill he took was a daily multivitamin.

Stress

Having ruled out a general medical condition, prescription medications, street drugs, and alcohol as the cause of George's depression, I next inquired about recent stressful events with the following question: "I'd like to go back to the question your family doctor asked you. He asked if you have any relationship problems or problems at work and you answered,

'Just the usual.' I want to make certain that you are not minimizing any problem, so I'm asking you to say more about 'just the usual' problems."

George said, "Oh. You know. Things like employees arguing. That's always been a problem and always will be. That's just part of running a company. But, no, nothing unusual there. My company is doing great. My home life? Well, my wife is a fine person, but there is a little tension between us because I'm so blah, so unresponsive. She takes it personally. Thinks it's her fault. I can understand why she feels that way. But I don't think the friction between us is causing my depression. Just the reverse. It's my depression that's causing the tension between us. Actually, I have less stress now than ever before, and yet my depression is worse."

From what George had told me, I was not able to identify any recent stress as the main causes of his depression. Next, I turned my attention to his childhood past.

Childhood Loss

A person who has lost a parent before age ten is often susceptible to depression in adult life.[1-3] Therefore I asked George, "Did you lose either of your parents, or anyone else who was close to you, when you were a child?"

George shook his head no. "Dad died fifteen years ago," he said. "Cancer of the pancreas. Mom died nine years ago from heart disease."

Physical and Sexual Abuse

Adults who have been sexually or physically abused as children are more susceptible than most people to depression. Many abused children believe it was their fault, and memories of the offending adult are accompanied by intense feelings of despair. Whether a person has been abused as a child usually cannot be ascertained early during psychotherapy, as it is too painful and frightening for the patient to remember. A few patients do remember such incidents but are too embarrassed to talk about them.

I did not want to be too direct in my questions about such matters lest George experience me as intrusive and not respectful of his boundaries. Instead I made a general statement, "Problems during childhood are often forgotten but leave emotional scars that can contribute to depression. Psychotherapy, or 'talking therapy' as it is commonly known, is often used to find out about such potential problems. Let's discuss that later."

Genetic Factors

Scientific evidence suggests that genes may make a person more vulnerable to depression. Studies have shown that a person with a blood relative who is depressed is at an increased risk of depression.[4–5] When an identical twin becomes depressed, there is a high probability that the other twin will become depressed also, which indicates a genetic component predisposes a person to depression. But the identical twin does not always become depressed, which indicates that environment does play a role in causing depression.

I had suspected for a long time that there is a genetic connection between alcoholism and depression, as both seem to run in families.[6–7] Moreover, the same *type* of depression seems to run in families. In George's case, I wondered if either of his parents had atypical depression.

When I asked him if either of his parents had an excessive appetite and tended to put on weight, he seemed uncomfortable, squirmed, and answered, "I think Mom did. At least she was hungry all the time like me. She said she could gain weight just by looking at food. I'm not sure about Dad. I've often wondered if he was depressed and that's why he drank. I'm not sure."

I said to George, "From what you've told me about you parents' alcoholism and your mother's depression, I suspect you are predisposed to depression, to atypical depression in particular. Just how this predisposition might work to partially cause your depression is unknown, but you may have an inherited gene that causes a chemical imbalance in your brain. That doesn't mean that a gene is the sole cause of your depression. It simply means that you may be more likely to become depressed when confronted with life's stresses."

Summary of Possible Causes for George's Depression

As our second session was drawing to a close, I said to George, "I think you're suffering from atypical depression, but I don't know what is causing it. We have ruled out adverse reaction to presciption medications, alcohol, drugs, and recent stress as possible causes. Based on what you told me about the exam by your family physician, we can assume your depression is not caused by a general medical condition."

George responded, "I'd like to interrupt. I beg to differ with you. We think we've ruled out a physical or chemical cause of my depression, but

I'm not so sure. Just because we haven't found a physical cause doesn't mean that there isn't one. I still think something is wrong with me physically, with my body."

"I stand corrected. You are making an excellent point," I replied. "It would have been better if I had said, 'Within the limits of what we now know about you, we cannot find a medical disease as an explanation.' Let's keep an open mind that an unknown physical disorder may be causing your depression. For shorthand we can refer to the unknown factor as 'Factor X'. Does this sound reasonable to you?"

George answered that it did. I continued, "As far as I can determine, the most likely causes of your depression are genetic factors that predispose you to atypical depression, painful childhood incidents—some of which you may not remember—and there may be an X factor."

Our time was running out, so we made another appointment for three days later. I told George I wanted to discuss treatment plans during our next session, if that was agreeable with him. He agreed, and our second session came to a close.

CHAPTER 4

Formulating
a Treatment Plan

*The relationship between doctor and patient . . . has been
designated as the art; yet I wonder whether it should not,
most properly, be called the essence.*
—WARFIELD T. LONGCOPE (1887–1953), *professor of medicine
and physician-in-chief at Johns Hopkins Hospital*

*Never forget that it is not a pneumonia,
but a pneumonic man who is your patient.
Not a typhoid fever, but a typhoid man.*
—WILLIAM WITHEY GULL (1816–1890), *influential humanistic English physician*

At the beginning of our next session, I told George I was able to describe the type of depression he had, namely atypical depression, but that I did not know what was causing his depression, and moreover, treatment was uncertain. I told him I wanted to discuss various forms of treatment, including psychotherapy, exercise, diet, and possibly medication.

Psychotherapy ("Talk Therapy")

I explained, "I *always* recommend some type of psychotherapy as part of the treatment plan for someone who is depressed. The type of talk therapy I practice is psychoanalysis and a less intensive form of psychoanalysis known as psychoanalytic psychotherapy. I always want to find out how the past shapes a person's current life. During our first meeting, you told me you had spoken with several psychotherapists, but that didn't help. Is that correct?"

George agreed, "Yes. They helped me cope, but they didn't help me get to the bottom of the problem. I don't think it was their fault. Maybe I'm too impatient. I quit because I didn't think we were getting anywhere. Plus my family thinks seeing a psychiatrist and being depressed is a sign of weakness. On some level, I guess I agree with them."

I told George, "I'm aware of the prejudice that depression afflicts only the weak, but I disagree with that opinion. I've seen hundreds of wonderful, fine, strong depressed people who I was able to help. Of course I can't tell you about them, but I can tell you that many famous people throughout history have been depressed. Both Abraham Lincoln and Eleanor Roosevelt struggled with depression, as did Winston Churchill. Several modern public figures, including the author William Styron, newscaster Mike Wallace, and humorist Art Buchwald, have suffered from depression. They have made their suffering public knowledge in order to get the message across to the public that depression is a recognized, treatable medical illness, just like pneumonia or a broken leg. I hope your bias against seeing a psychiatrist doesn't prevent you from giving it a try with me. I'm almost positive that talk therapy will help you, but I'm not sure it will get to the basic cause of your depression. I have, however, seen many patients over the years whose depression lifted with psychotherapy alone."

Exercise

I said to George, "At least two scientific studies have shown that exercise, such as walking briskly or jogging, for thirty minutes three times a week is as helpful in relieving depression as are antidepressant medications.[1–2] But, as you told me during our first meeting, you are too tired now to exercise as much as you want to and need to."

George responded, "I read about that study in the newspaper. I think you are referring to the study done right over here at Duke [University Medical Center] on exercise as a treatment of depression. Exercise has helped me keep my head above water. It does help my depression. No doubt about that. I still try to force myself to exercise some, but the problem now is that I'm so exhausted I have trouble exercising as much as I need to. And my muscles ache after I exercise."

I said, "Hopefully, after we work together for a while, you'll feel less depressed and will be able to exercise more. I'm not recommending exercise as the sole treatment. It's just a part of a total plan."

Diet

Next I told George, "Some evidence suggests that people whose diets are deficient in fish (a source of omega-3 fatty acids) are at increased risk of developing depression, so I recommend supplementing your diet with fish oil.[3–4] The increased consumption of sugar and flour products (refined carbohydrates) in the twentieth century has been linked with a corresponding increase in depression, along with diseases of the heart and blood vessels, and diabetes.[5] Results of epidemiological studies (the study of disease in populations), however, must be interpreted cautiously, as there are many confounding variables. Nevertheless, I recommend a diet low in whatever tastes sweet, low in rapidly absorbed carbohydrates such as potatoes and white bread, low in animal fat, and high in protein as part of a treatment plan for depression. A good rule of thumb is not to eat anything that is white, which includes many carbohydrates such as sugar, white bread, pasta, and rice. Obviously there are exceptions such as cauliflower, egg whites, and many kinds of fish and seafood."

George answered, "Thank you for your thoroughness and for telling me about that, but actually I'm already following most of your dietary recommendations."

Antidepressant Medications

I explained, "There is a class of antidepressant medications known as monoamine oxidase inhibitors [MAOIs] that are effective and specific for your type of depression. I do not, however, recommend them as a first-line treatment because of their side effects and because I prefer to know more about you and employ conservative measures before prescribing any antidepressant medication.

"There are other classes of antidepressant medications known as tricyclics such as Sinequan, and selective serotonin reuptake inhibitors or SSRIs like Prozac, Paxil, and Zoloft, but they are not as effective as MAOIs—like Nardil—for your type of depression.[6–11]

"The tricyclics and SSRIs are effective—and often life-saving—for some people, especially those whose depression comes on fast over a few days or weeks, is severe, and who have lost weight, have no appetite, can't sleep, are morbidly self-critical, and who have suicidal thoughts. But that's not the type of depression you have. Unfortunately antidepressant medications are prescribed too often and for disorders for which they were never intended."

I added, "You told me in our first meeting that you don't want to take an antidepressant medication. I don't want to prescribe one either, at least not until I get to know you. But let's keep an open mind. If your depression doesn't lift after a period of insightful psychotherapy, at some point we should reconsider medication." George agreed.

Summary of Treatment Suggestions for George

As our third meeting was drawing to a close, I said to George, "I know what type of depression you have, but unfortunately I don't know its exact cause. To try to find out, I recommend that we start with a course of psychotherapy for you. Also, I suggest you continue to exercise as much as you can, and continue to eat a low-carbohydrate diet, supplement it with omega-3 fatty acids and the vitamins and minerals you are taking."

George responded, "I'm not so sure about psychotherapy. I'll have to think about all that. I do like you and I can see how thorough you are. I do want to come back and talk to you again."

We scheduled a meeting for three days later.

I had made a diagnosis to the best of my ability, which was atypical depression of unknown cause, and had suggested a course of treatment for George. While making a correct diagnosis is imperative, treatment of depression or any emotional difficulty is not just about making the correct diagnosis and prescribing the right treatment. Nor is it about systematically "cutting into" someone's life story with a few pointed questions here and there. Psychotherapeutic treatment involves listening—really listening—to that "voice of mystery" in every human being. And through that listening, coming to see the beautiful complexity in each person. I hoped I would have that opportunity with George.

CHAPTER 5

Taking the Back Roads

Poets and philosophers before me discovered the unconscious;
what I discovered was the scientific method by which
the unconscious can be studied.

—SIGMUND FREUD (1856–1939)
Viennese physician and founder of psychoanalysis

As I waited for George, I wondered about him as a person. Who had loved him deeply? Or had *anyone* ever loved him deeply? Whom had he turned to for help when he needed it, or *had* there been anyone there to turn to? What were his life aspirations when he was age ten, twenty, and thirty? What disappointments had he suffered? Whom had he loved and whom had *he* disappointed? Did he have any regrets, any sorrows?

I heard the waiting room door open, indicating that George had arrived for our fourth session. He came into my office and sat down.

George began our session by saying, "You recommended psychotherapy during our last session. Before I decide anything, I want to ask you some questions about it."

Learning about Psychotherapy

"Of course, go ahead," I replied. "I hope I can answer them."

George leaned forward and spoke, "Do you really think psychotherapy can help me? I don't want to sound like a complainer and so negative, but I've felt bad and been depressed for so many years. I can't help being pessimistic. I know you think talking about my problems will probably work or you wouldn't be recommending it, but I guess I need to hear it from you."

I answered, "Almost all people with depression can be helped."

He responded, "During our last meeting, you told me about the famous people who have been helped by seeing a psychiatrist. Were those people treated with psychotherapy?"

"That's a good question. I don't know exactly what treatment they received or what type of depression they had. But I can tell you that almost all of my patients have found that psychotherapy helped their lives in general. In addition to psychotherapy, some of them have required antidepressant medications. I don't know for certain if psychotherapy will help your depression, but it will increase your self-awareness and perhaps help in unexpected ways. I think you should give it a try."

After a few moments, George asked, "How long will it take?"

"I don't know how long we'll need to meet together," I said. "There is no hard and fast rule. I intend to be here as long as it takes, for as long as we both feel it is necessary. We can evaluate how much psychotherapy helps you as we go forward, after you learn more about yourself."

George said, "If I'm hearing you right, I think you're saying the proof of the pudding is in the taste? We'll have to give it the test of time and see if it works. Well, that sounds reasonable. But tell me more about this process. What does it involve? I know it's 'talk therapy' but I don't know exactly what you mean by the kind of psychotherapy you do."

I explained, "Analytically oriented psychotherapy is a form of talking therapy which is based on the principles of psychoanalysis. It is a reverie, a study of daydreams and night dreams, of your reactions to me, of your past and present, and where the past and present meet. It is just as important to know what psychotherapy is *not*.

"Psychotherapy is not about giving you advice, trying to alter your behavior without understanding motivations, or actively telling you how to cope with specific situations. The *purpose* of it is to gain insight—it's often called insight-oriented psychotherapy—into childhood events that live on in the unconscious part of your mind and might be causing or contributing to your depression.

"I am positive about one thing. Our past is *always* living in the present. It's not a matter of whether or not past events shape our current life. It's a matter of *to what degree* the past affects our current relationships, as well as our feelings about ourselves."

George then asked, "What do I do in psychotherapy?"

"Just say whatever comes to your mind," I answered. "Allow your thoughts and feelings to ramble, regardless of whether or not they seem significant or pleasant or unpleasant. I will listen attentively and try to understand what in your unconscious is contributing to your emotional difficulties."

George objected, "Just letting my mind ramble seems like a waste of time. That goes against the grain for me. I'm impatient. I'm a get-it-done-now, no-bullshit type of person. In my work I focus on a problem and put everything else out of my mind. Just letting my mind ramble without any focus sounds lazy to me. I don't buy it. How can that help?"

I answered, "Apparently that style has helped you in your profession, but that's not the best way to conduct psychotherapy. Let me try to explain my view more fully. Suppose you were planning to take a trip by car and you had to choose between the Interstate and the back roads. My impression of you so far is that you'd take the Interstate, get in the left lane, and go eight miles per hour over the speed limit. You wouldn't take time to go to the bathroom unless absolutely necessary. All you would remember from the trip would be a blur of fast cars and eighteen-wheelers. That is not how psychotherapy works. If you took the back roads and drove slowly, can you imagine how much more you would see and experience? Maybe you would see hills with trees sprouting new leaves, farmers plowing their fields, foals galloping across a pasture, or dogs wagging their tails as children get off the school bus. And maybe seeing some of these things would remind you of something you did or experienced in the past."

To my surprise, George leaned forward, held his head in his hands, and began to sob. This moment moved me. I understood it as an indication that he trusted me enough to tell me how he was feeling through his tears. I remained silent until his crying stopped, and pointed to a box of tissues near at hand. This tough guy, this depression-fighter, dried his eyes with the back of his hands, as a child might and said, "I never took time for that sort of thing—smelling the roses. I'm so exhausted. I think it's time I did that. When can we start?"

I suggested we begin meeting once a week. "Once a week," I told him, "is not written in stone. If you need to meet more often, let's try to do that. I have an opening on Thursdays at 9:00 A.M. Can you make that?" George said that he could.

A most fascinating journey for George and me was about to begin. Or perhaps it had already begun.

CHAPTER 6

The Long Way Home

Memory is the only way home.

—Terry Tempest Williams (1955–)
author of Refuge: An Unnatural History of Family and Place

Before George's next session, I was anticipating his arrival and wondered where psychotherapy would take us. I hoped it would help George as much as it had helped many of my depressed patients. For me, psychotherapy has always been an inspiring process that is full of surprises. I looked forward to beginning this course with George and wondered what surprises would unfold.

Next Session

As soon as George sat down in my office, he asked, "Where should I begin?"

I answered, "I'd like you to choose the topic so that I can learn what's on your mind. I encourage you to speak as freely as possible about anything. Think of yourself as the teacher and me as your pupil. Teach me about yourself."

George began, "On the way over here this morning I was thinking about Dad and his drinking problem, and what effect it has had on me."

"Hmmm," I uttered. "Please say more."

George took a deep breath and continued, "Dad was my hero. I remember sitting in the bay window looking down the street and waiting for him to come home. Waiting and waiting. And then around the corner he came. His head was bent forward and his elbows were pointed out and were swaying from side to side, like a hockey player skating. He'd taken me to a couple of hockey games by then. I was so happy to see him. I thought Dad was acting like a hockey player, and then I heard Mom scream, 'Oh no. Not again.' I didn't understand it at the time, but later I realized Dad was drunk. He disappointed me so many times."

George and I sat silently for a few moments as he tried to stifle tears. When he was composed, I asked, "How old were you then?"

He replied, "Four or five, maybe six."

I wondered how his disappointment would play out in his relationship with me; that is, in the transference, as it is called in psychoanalysis. Would George experience me as a disappointing father? And if he did, what reactions would he have? How would he handle it? How would I handle it? Or, better yet, how would *we* handle it? It seemed premature for me to ask these questions aloud, but I would remember them, and I thought we would return to them at some future time. Instead I asked, "How do you think your father's alcoholism has shaped how you behave and feel today?"

George answered, "I couldn't depend on him. I learned to do everything myself."

I wanted to learn to what extent his fear of disappointment shaped his current life, so I asked, "Can you tell me about a recent situation when you felt as though you could not depend on others?"

George paused then spoke, "Well, at work I have trouble delegating responsibility. I take on too much myself. I do things that others are capable of doing. I'm a micro-manager. In the Adult Children of Alcoholics group I attended, they told me my behavior is typical for children of alcoholics. Taking on too much myself not only hurts me, it doesn't let my employees grow by dealing with challenges. If I could let them do more, my company would be even better, and I wouldn't have to work so hard."

A few sessions later, George's tendency to take too much on his own shoulders became apparent in the relationship with me.

He seemed impatient and stated, "I'm not making as much progress as I'd like. It's my fault. Tell me what more I can do."

I counseled patience but moments later realized I had missed the point. My comment to George expressed distance, a rejection of sorts. The point was, he had left me out of the equation. Just as he had to function without help for much of his life, he was assuming the same with me.

I told George, "You say *you* need to work harder. You left me out.

This is a *we* process, a two-person process. It's mutual. You don't seem to expect me to carry my weight."

George responded, "Funny you should say that. I have no reason to doubt you're reliable. My family doctor told me you are. I wouldn't be here if I thought you weren't. But every time I drive into your parking lot, I always look to see if your car is here. When I see it, I'm surprised it's there, and I feel relieved."

I made the interpretation to George that he expected me to disappoint him as his father had done, which is an example of transference. Transference happens in ordinary life, as well as in psychoanalysis and psychotherapy. We transfer our past experiences onto the present. If, for example, three people are rude to us in one day, we might expect the fourth to be rude also.

George found this interpretation enlightening. Over time, he gradually began to trust me. We developed a close professional relationship (or "therapeutic alliance" as it is known in psychotherapy) based on our growing mutual respect and understanding of our roles in psychotherapy. George said he felt a sense of comfort as he anticipated our sessions. At last he didn't have to carry the entire burden himself.

In later sessions, George shifted the focus to his mother, "I feel she had more of a relationship with alcohol than with me. I think that caused me to be overly sensitive to rejection. I'm likely to overreact to imagined slights from women. I'm so afraid they'll reject me that I'm not able to be the boss at work and insist on high performance of the women at work. I let them get away with murder. Just last week an irate customer called me and said he had called at 8:10 A.M.—we're supposed to open at 8:00 A.M.—but no one answered the phone. I apologized and told him I'd take care of it myself. What I should have done was chew out my employee and insist she get to work on time. She's a little older than me and has been with me a long time. I do care about her. She reminds me of Mom. I'm afraid she won't like me if I say anything critical to her."

Many sessions later, he experienced me as if I were his mother, an example of maternal transference.

One morning he complained, "Your office is a little messy. Too much clutter. Annoys me. I go to the other extreme. I'm too neat and orderly."

"Does my messy office bring back any memories?" I asked.

George answered, "Yes. I remember when Mom would get more depressed and start drinking, the house would become a wreck. I'd scurry around trying to keep things in order. I couldn't control Mom's behavior and was afraid to say anything to her about it, but at least I could try to keep the place neat."

I asked, "I wonder if you were afraid to tell me about your irritation with me, afraid I'd reject you rather than try to understand you?"

George looked surprised. "Yes. It's [the messy office] been irritating me for some time, but I never mentioned it. Guess I was afraid you'd stop trying to help me."

As the psychotherapy sessions continued, George and I had several occasions of illumination similar to those described above—moments that were deeply moving for both of us. Sigmund Freud wrote to Wilhelm Fleiss, a Berlin physician with whom Freud often collaborated, that such moments are indescribably beautiful. After such occasions of understanding with George, the tension in the room suddenly seemed to diminish as we both felt relief and closeness in understanding. Our relationship grew stronger.

Based on his increased understanding of how his past lived on in the present and distorted his perceptions, George was eventually able to change his maladaptive behavior toward both women and men. He was able to insist that women employees meet high standards, and was able to delegate more responsibility to male employees. His successful business became even more successful. And his behavior toward his wife changed. For many years he had become angry with her if someone else made her laugh. On such occasions he would become silently angry and withdraw from her. After many sessions had passed, he realized that he had perceived his wife as if she were his mother. He became less sensitive to real and imagined slights by her. When they had a disagreement, he was able to calmly tell her about his feelings rather than "let it build up inside and later explode." Their relationship improved.

George repeated in several sessions how thrilled and grateful he was for the insights he had gained and the *behavioral* changes he had made. But, his *feelings* of depression, tiredness, and hunger persisted.

Initially, I thought George's depression had not lifted because of unresolved unconscious conflicts and guilt. Was he angry with his parents, but turned that anger on himself so as not to alienate them? Was he guilty because he was more successful than his father had ever been? Did he feel guilty and depressed because he had occasionally hated his father? Did he want to punish me by refusing to feel better? Or did he feel self-critical and depressed because he hated his mother?

George and I discussed these and other possibilities, but his depression refused to yield to further insights.

During one session, I asked George to summarize his opinion of our work together up to this point.

He said, "I wouldn't take a million dollars for what I've learned about myself with your help. It's allowed me to make a lot of changes. But it hasn't helped my depression. In spite of all we've talked about here, and how much better things are going, I'm still depressed. I'm still tired. And I'm still hungry all the time. I overeat and feel guilty about that. And I don't sleep well—I toss and turn all night and am sleepy in the morning and mentally dull."

As this session was drawing to a close, I told George not to despair and reminded him of my recommendation during our third meeting, which was that if he continued to be depressed after a period of illuminating psychotherapy, we should consider an antidepressant medication in addition to ongoing psychotherapy.

George commented, "Sounds reasonable. I'll think about it. See you next time."

CHAPTER 7

Murder of the Senses: A Trial of an Antidepressant Medication

The drug he gave me, which he said was precious and cordial to me, have I not found it murd'rous to th' senses?

—WILLIAM SHAKESPEARE (1564–1616)

In our next session, I told George it was clear to me that he needed more than psychotherapy and I told him *why* I thought he should give antidepressant medications a try. Despite an insightful period of psychotherapy—his depression, tiredness, hunger, and restless sleep persisted. This suggested to me that some underlying biological imbalance was contributing to his depression, and it was not responding to talk therapy.

George answered, "I'll agree to take an antidepressant because you know me so well and because I've learned so much from you. If you had proposed that after only a session or two, I wouldn't be here now. Do you really believe it will help me?"

I told him, "I can't be certain of that. As I mentioned briefly in an earlier session, there is no safe antidepressant medication that the FDA has approved for your type of [atypical] depression. The class of antidepressants that is the most effective for atypical depression—known as MAOIs—can react with certain foods and cold medications to cause dangerous, even fatal, side effects. Therefore, they are rarely prescribed."[1–2]

George asked, "Like what kind of foods?"

"Bananas, yeast breads, many types of aged cheese, broad beans, beef and chicken livers, sour cream, chocolate—"

George interrupted me. "You don't need to go on. That list is already too long. I'm not going to take that medication."

"You're like most people," I agreed. "You don't want to take a MAOI. There is a newer class of antidepressants known as SSRIs—such as Prozac, Paxil, and Zoloft—that you could try. There is some evidence that they may be effective in atypical depression, but unfortunately, they too have side effects.[3–7] They're just not as dangerous as MAOI side effects."

George asked, "What are the SSRI side effects?"

I answered, "They can include feeling emotionally flat or numb, upset stomach, weight gain, ringing in the ears, electricity-like sensations under the skin of the arms and legs, and the most common and most frequently and undesirable reported side effect in my practice is impairment of sexual life. Whether you will get those side effects, I don't know. Unfortunately, it may require trial and error."

George reluctantly agreed to start taking one of the newer antidepressants. I had some samples of Zoloft and gave them to him.

He said, "OK, let's give Zoloft a try."

Taking an Antidepressant

In late winter of 1992, some ten months into our weekly psychotherapy sessions, George started taking 100 milligrams of Zoloft per day. He said he felt relaxed and revitalized after taking Zoloft for only three or four days.

He reported, "Since taking Zoloft, I'm able to enjoy life more. I was mowing the grass yesterday, and the newly cut grass smelled fresh and appeared lusciously green. After I finished, I took a shower and the water running down my back felt so pleasant. And I'm not as anxious, either."

We were both delighted with his positive response to Zoloft. Unfortunately, George's improvement lasted less than two weeks, at which point his depression, tiredness, and hunger began to return. Again, nothing brought him pleasure.

He felt very disappointed and so was I. The lack of sustained improvement in his mood was another in a series of disappointments he had undergone in his life. For a few days, George thought he had found a remedy for a depression that had plagued him for so many years, but his progress seemed to be slipping away.

I told him I could understand his distress, and suggested that his failing response to medication might simply be a result of too small a dose. We increased his dosage to 150 milligrams per day. This improved his depression, but within one week he developed several unpleasant side effects.

George enumerated his symptoms: "I have diarrhea, and I feel slowed down physically and mentally. My ears are ringing. It [Zoloft] has killed my sexual sensations, and it has taken away my drive to succeed. I feel blah."

It was clear to both of us that at 150 milligrams per day, the side effects outweighed the benefits. Eventually, we settled on a dosage of 125 milligrams per day. George reported that he still had the same side effects and they were still quite disagreeable to him, but this dosage improved his symptoms "about 60 to 70 percent" and therefore he could tolerate them "at least for awhile."

By this time, George and I had been meeting weekly for almost a year.

He lamented, "I feel life is behind me. The side effects of Zoloft, especially feeling slowed down and drugged, continue to annoy me. I don't know how much longer I'm willing to take it. I'm really disappointed. For a few days I had a glimpse of what life could be like without depression."

"I do understand," I answered. "I'm disappointed too, however, I recommend that you continue taking 125 milligrams of Zoloft per day for a while longer, and let's continue our weekly psychotherapy meetings in the hope that your symptoms will lift and your side effects will lessen. Zoloft may not be the right drug for you and if you don't feel better soon, we should switch to another antidepressant."

His condition did not improve. If anything, it became worse. Each time when I went to the waiting room to invite him into my office, his countenance was the same: he wore a frown, and he walked into my office very slowly and sat down heavily. For George, life was an uphill climb with a cold wind in his face. Although he had resolved not to commit suicide, he felt as if his life was behind him. As he stated, "My emotional life is dead. I'm just waiting for my body to catch up."

PART TWO

Finding One of Nature's Secrets

CHAPTER 8

A Ray of Light

I feel great!
—GEORGE

One day, a little more than a year after George and I had started meeting together, he greeted me in the waiting room with a boyish, almost mischievous, grin on his face instead of his usual downcast look. Instead of walking slowly into my office with his shoulders stooped, he stood tall and had a slight spring in his step.

As he sat down, he smiled and said, "I feel great!"

I couldn't believe what I was seeing and hearing.

George continued, "There is something I am embarrassed to tell you. I feel so gullible. Several months ago, a neighbor of mine asked me to join a multi-tiered organization that sells health supplements. You know, the type of sales organization where the more people you recruit, the more money you make. A pyramid scheme. I don't believe in such organizations. I've never belonged to one and never will.

"But some months ago, I did start taking some of the vitamin and mineral pills he gave me. I felt so bad I was willing to try almost anything. I didn't notice any effect so I never mentioned it to you, since we had so much else to talk about.

"Last week he gave me some new pills, a dietary supplement that I'd never taken before. He said they might control my appetite and help me lose weight. Well, of course that got my interest. Within three days after taking them I felt wonderful—better than I've felt since I was eighteen years old. I can't believe it. I have a lot more energy. I'm not as hungry as

I used to be. And—what I really can't believe—is that I'm not depressed. My thinking is sharp. It's amazing. I don't know what to think of it.

"It's like I've been a prisoner in my own body, weighted down by a ball and chain for all these years before, and now I'm free."

A Manic Episode?

I didn't believe George's improvement was due to the supplement. Rather, I was immediately concerned that Zoloft was causing him to become manic.

A person having a manic episode is abnormally elated, talks excessively and unintelligibly, cannot sleep, is uncontrollably aggressive, and has inappropriate sexual behavior. These symptoms last for a week or longer. Mania can be triggered in susceptible people by all antidepressant medications, including Zoloft.

A manic episode is a true medical emergency, and the person often requires hospitalization.

I saw one particularly memorable incident of mania over thirty years ago. Soon after I had opened my practice, a pediatrician asked if I would see one of his patients. The doctor described his patient as a formerly robust seventeen-year-old boy who was having crying spells and losing weight, and had recently dropped out of high school. I called the number given me. The boy's father answered. I introduced myself and offered an appointment time for his son. As I began giving directions to my office, the father interrupted me and said that his son was too weak to get out of bed. He asked if I would make a house call. I agreed, but wondered why, from the pediatrician's description, the boy was so weak. Later that day, when I arrived at the boy's home and was walking toward the door, both parents rushed out to greet me. They were visibly distressed and thanked me profusely for coming to see their son at home. They led me to a back bedroom where their son lay. It was a shocking sight.

The young boy looked as if he was a terminally ill person. He was emaciated and was trembling all over, as if about to freeze, though the day was extremely hot. He whimpered, as if too weak to cry loudly. His parents indicated he had lost about thirty pounds in a few weeks. When asked why they had not sought psychiatric care sooner, they stammered and said something like, "Well, he is a popular kid, and, uh, well you know, what would the other kids think?" I recommended hospitalization, but for reasons I cannot now recall, that didn't happen. I prescribed Elavil, an older form of antidepressant medication. The next day I made another house call. He was feeling better. Three days later he was deliriously happy, singing loudly, and talking so fast I was unable to understand him. He was intermittently combative, and slept only three to four hours a night, if that long. His condition worsened and developed into a manic psychosis with hallucinations and delusions. He required hospitalization and was later treated with lithium (a mood-stabilizing metallic element), which eventually restored his psychological equilibrium.

In order to rule out the possibility that George himself might be experiencing a manic episode, I asked him if he felt extremely "high" or if he were staying up all night.

He answered, "No. I know what you're getting at. You think I might be manic. I saw a man become manic in a group I was in once. You're wondering if I'm too high, too 'up,' and out of control. I'm not. And I've been sleeping well every night."

George was not having an antidepressant-induced manic episode as I had suspected. Several other possible explanations came to my mind, including serotonin syndrome, a placebo response, or a "flight into health," a type of placebo response in which the patient "runs" from problems rather than attempting to understand them.

Serotonin Syndrome?

My next step was to rule out the possibility that George might be having what is called "serotonin syndrome." While too little serotonin in the brain can cause depression, too much serotonin in the brain, caused by antidepressant medications, can be a serious, even fatal condition known as serotonin syndrome. The symptoms of serotonin syndrome are: feeling excessively happy for no apparent reason, feeling or acting as if happily drunk, agitation, dizziness, confusion, sweating, stiff muscles, jerky movements, shakiness of the hands, lack of coordination, nausea, high blood pressure, loss of consciousness, and death.[1-3] I observed George carefully for signs of serotonin syndrome, but he was not shaky or trembling, he was not sweating, his muscles were not twitching, and he was not confused or nauseated. George did not show the symptoms of serotonin syndrome.

A Placebo Response?

Having ruled out an antidepressant-induced manic episode and serotonin syndrome, I turned my attention to the possibility that George had a placebo response to the supplement he had taken. This is a response based on hope and desperation rather than to a specific response to a medication. I recalled the Russian novelist Alexander Solzhenitsyn's beautiful description of the motivations for a placebo response in his book, *Cancer Ward*:

> *Whether they [cancer patients] admit it as much or denied it,*
> *they all without exception in the depths of their hearts believed*
> *that there was a doctor, or a[n] herbalist, or some old witch of a*
> *woman somewhere, whom you only had to find and get that*
> *medicine . . . to be saved . . . It just wasn't possible that their*
> *lives were already doomed. However much we laugh at miracles*
> *when we are strong, healthy, and prosperous, if life becomes so*
> *hedged and cramped that only a miracle can save us, then we*
> *clutch at this unique, exceptional miracle and—believe in it!*

I had seen countless examples of the placebo response in my practice. An anxious patient, for example, made an appointment with me and arrived at our first appointment *already* feeling calm. A depressed man felt better after I gave him a prescription but *before* he began taking the medication. I could cite many more examples, as the placebo response is so common.

The placebo effect is not limited to medicine or psychiatry. All of us have it at one time or another. For instance, we can be fraught with anxiety when a car battery dies and we are stranded on the highway at night, but feel immediate relief after knowing that competent help is on the way.

The Good and Bad of the Placebo Response

The placebo response is not always a helpful one. It is good when it augments the specific, biological effects of a medication or treatment. For example, a person may be hospitalized with pneumonia but may feel better temporarily before the antibiotic is taken or has a chance to be effective. The reason is that the feeling of hope reduces stress, and causes various other chemical changes in the body that aid healing. These effects are even stronger if the patient has a good relationship with the physician and has been helped by him or her in the past. So far, so good.

But a problem arises when a person's placebo response masks an underlying disease and causes him or her to postpone or even refuse evidence-based, specific treatment. This wish-induced improvement can lull the person into thinking that he or she is actually better. Meanwhile the underlying untreated disease or medical condition often worsens—sometimes with fatal results.

Whereas the placebo response can cause temporary relief, ultimately, it is no substitute for a specific treatment for a specific illness. A placebo response typically fails the test of time and the symptoms return.

Was George Having a Placebo Response?

After ruling out a manic episode and serotonin syndrome, I thought a placebo response was the most likely explanation for George's improvement.

What was I to do next? As I've often done when confronted with uncertainty in a clinical situation, I asked myself what Sigmund Freud might have done in a similar situation—when faced, for example, with a patient who had a placebo response after taking a phony remedy from someone who might be labeled a charlatan.

I recalled reading Freud's words, which I paraphrase: 'Rather than dismiss a patient's response to a charlatan, we should try to understand his [that is, the charlatan's] appeal.'

So I began to study what I assumed was a placebo response. Obviously, I couldn't interview George's neighbor. I could, however, ask about his neighbor and I did. George knew little about him. He did not describe his neighbor as a charismatic, high-pressure salesman, the type one might expect could induce a placebo response. Next I asked him to bring to me any promotional literature that advertised the benefits of the pills.

He responded, "I'm glad you're going to examine them. I'm positive that the pills are responsible for how great I feel. But on the negative side, anything that powerful can also be dangerous."

I told George I agreed with him, and my first priority was to evaluate the pills for safety.

CHAPTER 9

A Miracle in Nature

All herbs are edible, but some only once.

—CROATIAN PROVERB

When I went out to greet George for our next session, he looked as bright as he did the session before. When I asked how he felt, he said, "Still great!" George handed me the pills that he felt had helped him, and the literature that was enclosed with the bottle.

Inflated Claims

As I read the exaggerated claims on the bottle label, the image of one of my medical school professors, Dr. Nathan Womack, flashed across my mind. Dr. Womack was chair of the Department of Surgery at the University of North Carolina School of Medicine. In one of his particularly vivid lectures he intended to open the eyes of medical students to the dangers of "quackery" and to the dangers of "medications" whose efficacy had not been proven according to the scientific method.

To an appreciative audience, Dr. Womack recounted an incident from his boyhood in the Midwest during the early 1900s. A "medicine" salesman came through town and parked his wagon in the middle of the dusty main street. He stood on the back of the wagon. People gathered around to hear what he had to say, and soon there was a large crowd. The salesman's pitch became more and more impassioned. Soon he worked the crowd into a frenzy. He promised them that his brand of medicine would cure dysentery, consumption (tuberculosis), arthritis, and even reverse the ravages of old age. And, to prove his point further, he added, "What I'm telling you is the gospel truth. But don't just believe me. Look right here. It's written right here on the bottle."

During the course of many years in practice, the wisdom of Dr. Womack and other teachers was reinforced as I saw many patients injured by unproven treatments. Itinerant salesmen have gone the way of the horse and buggy, but false claims for unproven health and medical products may actually be more problematic today. Television advertising and infomercials, Internet promotions, tabloid advertising, and other vehicles give legitimate and other marketers of, in some cases, questionable health-related products highly effective sales tools that reach tens of millions of people. And this market is arguably primed by many consumers who are frustrated with the shortcomings of the conventional, conservative, science-based medical approach, as well as with the high cost of pharmaceutical products.

Dangerous Side Effects of Some Herbs

I had planned to thoroughly read the promotional literature that George brought in after his session, but I wanted to briefly scan it while he was there. I asked if he minded if I glanced at it now and read it more thoroughly later. He agreed. As I scanned the label, I saw that the supplement contained many innocent vitamins, minerals, and amino acids, which are essential ingredients for normal functioning of the human body and have been tested for safety, but the supplement also contained herbs that might or might not have been tested for safety. The words "ephedra" and "kava" jumped off the label at me. I had read several reports of dangerous side effects caused by these herbs.

George correctly read my facial expression and commented, "You look worried and concerned."

"Yes. I am and I'm also angry," I answered. "The concoction you've been taking contains at least one herb, ephedra, that I suspect is dangerous. Also, it contains kava, which may be a dangerous herb. Because of this, I think you should stop taking the pills."

George sighed, then said, "You want me to stop taking the supplement that has helped me so much. Makes sense. I hate to in a lot of ways though because it has made me feel so much better. We'll see."

I told George I didn't expect any ill effects from his stopping the supplement, but to be on the safe side, I did warn him, "If you notice any significant change after you stop taking the pills, please let me know as soon as possible." He promised to do so.

George Stops the Supplement—Darkness Descends

George stopped the supplement after taking it each day for three weeks. He continued to take 125 milligrams (mg) of Zoloft per day. Seven days after stopping the pills, George sent me an e-mail that startled me and still startles me when I read it today. It read:

Dear Dr. McLeod,

I stopped taking everything last Sunday except Zoloft (125 mg). I still take three buffered salt tablets and one potassium tablet (99 mg) after I work out on the stairmaster for forty-five minutes.

Since this time (only one week), I have experienced the following:

1. Loss of energy.
2. Not sleeping well—waking up tired.
3. Sleeping until 7:00 A.M. instead of 6:00–6:30 A.M. Trouble getting out of bed.
4. Loss of muscle strength when working out on Nordic Flex Gold. Normally go forty-five minutes at level 9 on stairmaster. Could only go at level 9 for forty minutes, and five minutes at level 8—last ten minutes at level were a struggle.
5. More muscle tightness in neck and shoulders.
6. Bowel movements not as regular and harder. Dehydrated.
7. Frequent mild headaches.
8. Ringing in ears (that I've had since I started Zoloft) is louder.
9. Not as focused on anything. Have trouble concentrating.
10. Loss of desire for sex or anything—it doesn't matter if we do or if we don't do anything.

I'm not feeling pleasure in anything. I feel like I'm in a kind of a fog. This feels like mild depression, but without the feelings of hopelessness. I feel like I'm in a neutral gear going nowhere. And I don't seem to even care that I feel this way.

Hope this information helps!

George

I stared at these words on my computer screen in disbelief. I could hardly believe how severe George's symptoms were, and how fast they had returned after he had stopped taking the pills. He must be confused, I guessed, and had stopped Zoloft rather than the supplement.

I called George and told him I thought we should arrange a meeting as soon as possible.

He agreed to meet the next day.

When he entered my office the next day, he looked severely depressed, and his movements were slow. I asked him if he had mistakenly stopped Zoloft instead of the supplement.

He answered, "No. I'm still taking Zoloft. It's the supplement that I stopped. Two or three days after I stopped the supplement, I had a meeting with my accountants and attorneys, and I couldn't keep my mind on what they were saying. I couldn't concentrate on more than one line of thought. I think I managed to hide it from them, but my mind is not working right. Whatever was in that supplement helped me think clearly."

What did this mean? I was puzzled, just as I had been when George told me he had started taking the pills and felt so much better—better than he'd ever felt in his adult life—and now after stopping the pills, his depression had returned.

It seemed that the pills contained a powerful antidepressant agent. Was the antidepressant agent one of the herbs or one of the other hundred or so ingredients that were in the supplement?

The Choice Truths

As I considered the possibility, I was reminded of the words of Dr. John Morgan, an eighteenth-century physician and founder of America's first medical school: "The choice truths of Medicine are frequently blended with a heap of rubbish." Was there a "truth" in the pill George had taken that lifted depression, reduced carbohydrate craving, and improved concentration? How could I determine what was rubbish and what was the antidepressant ingredient? Were they different or the same?

Right away I sent an email to Dr. Robert N. Golden, chair of psychiatry at the University of North Carolina School of Medicine. Dr. Golden is a National Institute of Mental Health-trained researcher, and is highly regarded for his knowledge of psychopharmacology, which is the use of medication in the treatment of psychiatric disorders. In years past, whenever I was in doubt about what medication to prescribe for a patient, I always sought a second opinion from Dr. Golden.

In my email to Dr. Golden, I told him about this most remarkable occurrence—that depression had lifted in a man who had taken a dietary supplement containing many ingredients, and he had relapsed when the supplement was discontinued. I went on to say that I didn't know what to make of this. I had ruled out a manic episode and serotonin syndrome. A placebo response seemed more and more unlikely. I could find no explanation other than the pills contained an antidepressant agent, but I couldn't imagine what it might be.

Dr. Golden's reply was, "I don't believe it's the health pill either. Antidepressants just don't act that fast."

"What was I to do next?" I asked myself. I decided to take a long walk at lunchtime with the hope that I would get some sense of direction about this puzzling event.

CHAPTER 10

Needle in a Haystack

*Confronted with a multitude of different assumptions the mind
must guess the real nature of the concoction. Experiment . . .
by means of artificial, simplified combinations, discovers
the actual connection between the phenomena.*

—IVAN PAVLOV (1849–1936), *Russian neurophysiologist and behaviorist*

A s I walked at lunchtime, I thought of the challenges that faced
George and me. How could we find the proverbial needle in a
haystack? How could we identify the antidepressant ingredient in
the more than 100 possible ingredients in the supplement he had taken?

George had *not* responded to the first pills his neighbor gave him, but
he *had responded* to the second. This was the first clue. There must be an
ingredient that was present in the most recently taken pills (designated
here as supplement A) that was not present in the pills he had been taking
earlier (designated here as supplement B). Perhaps I could compare the
two supplements and find what supplement A contained that supplement
B did not. By this means, I might be able to narrow the list of suspects.

Comparison of Ingredients in the Two Supplements

When I returned to my office, I read the promotional literature distributed
with the concoction, this time more carefully. Both pills contained many of
the same ingredients, but in different amounts.

I compared the two supplements by using a spreadsheet to list all the
ingredients and do any necessary computations. In the first column of the

spreadsheet, I entered the names of all the ingredients in supplement A. In the next column, I entered the amount of each ingredient. In the third column, I entered the names of all ingredients in supplement B. In the fourth column, I entered the amounts of each ingredient in supplement B. In the last column, I calculated the percentage differences in the ingredients between the two pills.

I noticed that supplement A contained many herbs. Supplement B contained no herbs. This suggested that one of the herbs was the antidepressant ingredient. I continued, however, to look for other possibilities.

There was little difference in the amino acids and vitamins in the two mixtures, so I excluded them.

I did notice a difference in the trace minerals between supplements A and B. Although both supplements contained most of the same minerals, the minerals in supplement A were in the form of picolinates, that is, they were chelated (bound) to organic molecules, as for example, selenium picolinate. The minerals in supplement B were in the form of inorganic salts, as for example, selenium chloride.

Selection of Ingredients for Testing

By the method outlined above, I narrowed down the list to about twenty-five substances. How could I further narrow the list of herbs and trace minerals?

Herbs

I reasoned that if an herb had been responsible for George's dramatic relief from depression, it was likely that it would fall into the category of stimulating herbs, of which there were four in the pill: ephedra (or ma huang), kava, guarana (a natural source of caffeine), and ginseng.

For reasons mentioned in the preceding chapter, I did not want to give George ephedra or kava, as I believed them to be potentially harmful. This left two herbal suspects: ginseng and guarana. Some manufacturers claim ginseng helps people who have difficulty with concentration, hunger, and lack of energy—all symptoms that George had. Some people use guarana to get "high," as it contains a natural source of caffeine. Although St. John's wort was not contained in supplement A, I decided to include it because of widespread belief in its antidepressant effects.

Trace Minerals

To be thorough, I also wanted to consider trace elements or minerals as a possible explanation. Both sets of pills contained calcium, chromium, copper, selenium, manganese, molybdenum, vanadium, and zinc. But supplement A, which had helped George, contained all these minerals as picolinates and in much larger amounts than in supplement B. For example, supplement A contained selenium as selenium picolinate while supplement B contained selenium as selenium chloride. Also, supplement A contained chromium as chromium picolinate while supplement B contained chromium as chromic chloride.

To narrow down the list of trace minerals, I asked George to see his family physician and have his blood tested to determine if he had any trace mineral deficiency. He went the next day.

He received the results three days later. The blood test revealed that George had adequate amounts of calcium, copper, and zinc. However, no chromium, manganese, molybdenum, or vanadium was detected and only a miniscule amount of selenium was detected. The blood test thus narrowed down the list of mineral suspects to five, including selenium.

I did not know how to further narrow the list, as I knew little about trace minerals, so I read selected chapters in *Modern Nutrition in Health and Disease*.[1] This book is the most authoritative, comprehensive, up-to-date book on nutrition available. I also visited the website of the National Institutes of Health (NIH) Office of Dietary Supplements.[2]

From these sources I learned that essential minerals, such as selenium, chromium, magnesium, and zinc, are poorly absorbed by the body when in their inorganic or metallic forms. To aid in absorption, minerals are chelated (bound) with naturally occurring organic molecules, such as picolinic acid and niacin that aid in absorption by transporting minerals from the intestines into the body.

I learned that selenium is an antioxidant that prevents damage from free radicals. It's involved in the metabolism of the hormone-like substance, prostaglandin. Although selenium deficiency is rare in the United States, deficiency can cause abnormal development of the brain, as well as other disorders. Moreover, there was a report in the German literature that selenium lifts depression.[3] For these reasons, I selected selenium for the trial.

I learned that chromium is deficient in the modern man's diet and this deficiency can lead to impaired functioning of insulin and difficulty metabolizing ("burning") sugar and producing energy. People retain less chromium in the body as they age. Several studies suggested that chromium deficiency may contribute to heart disease and diabetes. The disorders associated with chromium deficiency are widespread and affect many parts of the human body. Chromium is thought to be one of the safest of essential trace minerals. For these reasons, it seemed logical to select it for the trial.

I was able to find very little about the role in metabolism of manganese, molybdenum, and vanadium, so I excluded them from the trial. I planned to test them later if none of the selected minerals was shown to be the active antidepressant agent.

Setting Up a Plan

I now had in mind the ingredients to test—guarana, ginseng, St. John's wort, chromium, and selenium.

To eliminate the placebo effect, I needed to choose a neutral substance. I selected vitamin C because it was not contained in either supplement A or B; it is widely taken; and it has no known effect on mood.

I told George about my comparison of the two supplements. I also told him that I had narrowed the list of suspects down to five, and proposed that we attempt to determine whether any of the five was the active ingredient in supplement A. The next step would be to give him each of these ingredients, one at a time, in a single-blind fashion—in other words, he would not know what ingredient he was taking, but I would.

George eagerly agreed to the following plan:

- I would give him six envelopes labeled "week #1" to "week #6." Each envelope would contain one of the five ingredients, or the placebo or "dummy pill."

- On the first Monday of the week, George would take one of the pills in the envelope marked "week #1" and take one pill each day for a total of five days. I had decided on the five-day schedule because he had responded to supplement A in less than a week and had relapsed in less than a week after its discontinuation.

- Each day, George would observe any reactions he might have whether mental or physical, and report them to me every day or two by email.

- On Fridays, he would fill out a self-rating scale to assess his mood. The scale I selected is a standard one used in psychiatric research and is called the "Symptom Check List 90," or SCL-90 for short. The SCL-90 is a self-rating scale composed of ninety questions designed to measure symptoms of excessive concern about one's body, obsessive-compulsive behavior, excessive sensitivity to rejection, depression, anxiety, hostility, phobic anxiety, suspiciousness, and being out of touch with reality.

- Throughout the seven-day week, George would continue taking 125 milligrams a day of Zoloft as usual.

This plan would continue for the next six weeks in the same manner, with George taking pills in envelopes labeled "week #2" the second week, "week #3" the third week, and so on. I thought it was imperative for me to check with an expert in the field of psychopharmacology to see if my plan sounded reasonable. I spoke with Dr. Golden—without revealing the identity of George—and told him about the plan of investigation I was considering. He thought the plan was a good one and advised me to make certain that I had fully informed George about the experimental nature of the proposed trial, which I had already done.

George was pleased by what he considered the "cleverness" of the plan and was eager to begin.

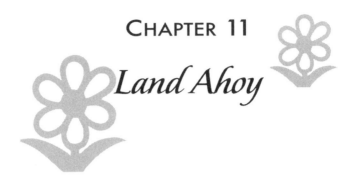

CHAPTER 11

Land Ahoy

[Columbus] enjoyed long stretches of pure delight such as
only a seaman may know, and moments of high
exultation that only a discoverer can experience.
—SAMUEL ELIOT MORISON (1887–1976), *leading American naval historian*

George began our single-blind trial the following Monday by taking the first of the pills in the envelope labeled "week #1." The course of the experiment is described below.

Week One

In the first week of the trial, George took 500 milligrams of vitamin C for five days beginning on Monday. I wondered if he would have a placebo response and in fact, he did. He felt better *before* he took the first vitamin C pill—presumably due to his hope for improvement of his depression.

On Tuesday, George reported by email: "I felt real good yesterday. . . . There is definitely a difference after taking the pills in the envelope marked 'week #1,' but not as much as before when I was taking supplement A."

On Wednesday, however, he reported, "The ringing in my ears is louder [a side effect previously experienced from taking Zoloft, which he was continuing to take], low energy—not out of energy—just not motivated to do much physically, more irritable than usual, still eating more than needed."

On the Thursday and Friday, George's condition continued to deteriorate. He wrote by email on Friday, "I still do not have any energy to do anything much. All I want to do is lie around and rest. I am in slow motion but I do not feel bad, only tired. It reminds me of when I first started taking 150 milligrams of Zoloft. Then I felt drugged and my mind worked very slow, just like the rest of my body. It's the same now. It's like being in molasses (mind and body) and being very slow."

On Friday, after taking 125 milligrams of Zoloft per day and 500 milligrams of vitamin C for one week, George filled out the SCL-90 self-rating scale, which is set up so that the answers range in severity from 0 (not at all) to 4 (extremely severe). The symptoms he rated as most troublesome were disturbed sleep, physical weakness, headache, low energy, overeating, poor memory, and loss of interest in life. A copy of that SCL-90 is on page 182.

George's placebo response had been short-lived, as is typical.

Week Two

The next week, George took 300 micrograms of chromium picolinate each of the five days.

On the evening of the first day, a Monday, George emailed me the following: "This morning I started the new pill, and this afternoon I have a lot more energy. It also seemed to be a little less than what I would like but a lot better than the last week. I was able to focus on things mentally better today than lately. My appetite seems to have disappeared. I ate normal meals but I did not rush to eat. I'm not hungry all the time. I don't know what I'm taking, but whatever it is, it is helping my body handle food, especially sugar. I do have a headache tonight, but I think I'm tired, as I have been more active today. I still have some ringing in my ears."

The next day, on Tuesday, George sent me the following email: "I rested very well last night and I dreamed more than usual. It was probably the most restful night's sleep that I have had in two weeks. Today I felt good physically and not as tired as I have been. I did, and do feel, a little down for some reason. I have virtually had no appetite today. When I ate, I did enjoy the meals. My energy is better. I worked out on my stairmaster when I got home and was able to do thirty minutes at level 9, five minutes at level 8, and ten minutes at level 7 for a grand total of forty-five minutes. I was unusually hot and flushed when I finished."

I was not able to comprehend George's rapid improvement after two days. He was obviously sleeping better, was not as tired or hungry, and had a lot more energy.

I was bewildered and incredulous. It couldn't be this simple.

I emailed Dr. Golden that chromium picolinate had helped a patient who had been suffering for years from atypical depression. I said that in the second week of the trial—after only one day—my patient's depressive symptoms had begun to lift. He had more energy, improved concentration, a decrease in appetite, and improved sleep. It appeared to me that the patient's improvement was due to chromium, but a more likely explanation was that something favorable had happened in his life recently that accounted for his dramatic improvement. I finished the email by saying that I would see George the next day in my office, and hopefully would find out some answers.

Dr. Golden responded by email and repeated, "Antidepressants just don't act that fast."

On Wednesday I saw George in my office. When I went to the waiting room to invite him in, I was surprised. The week before, he had appeared tense and grim, and had said he felt awful. Today he looked happy. His countenance reminded me of the day I saw him soon after he started dietary supplement A.

George said he felt much better. He added, "This is it. This is the one that helps me. I feel just as good as I did a few weeks ago when I took the supplement that made me feel so good."

I asked George if something favorable had happened in his personal life or business that might explain his improvement. He said there was nothing different. He was certain it was the pill at work.

George's improvement was corroborated by the SCL-90 that he completed at the end of the week. His answers to the SCL-90 on page 186 revealed almost complete relief of all his troublesome symptoms.

The difference in George's answers before and after taking chromium picolinate was astonishing. See page 190 for a graphic comparison of George's response to chromium.

Eureka!

For almost half a century, psychiatric researchers had been attempting, with little success, to find a method to speed up the onset of action of antidepressants. Might I have discovered such a method by chance? Was it possible that chromium picolinate could increase the efficacy of antidepressants and accelerate their onset of action? Often it takes as long as six weeks for antidepressant medications to relieve depression.

I sent another email to Dr. Golden that read, "Eureka! I think I have discovered a method of enhancing the efficacy of antidepressants, reducing side effects, and speeding up the onset of action. Nothing has occurred in my patient's life to account for his improvement. I can't believe this. If I can't believe it, I know no one else will. I'd like to have a member of the UNC staff, someone I don't know, interview my patient. He is quite willing to do this. And, by the way, it's going to be interesting to see if he does or does not respond to the other ingredients."

I doubt that Dr. Golden believed my findings either but, to his great credit, he continued to listen to me with an open mind, and he followed the trail of evidence as it emerged.

Week Three

George began taking 300 milligrams of guarana during the next five days. This amount of guarana contains 45 milligrams of a caffeine-like substance.

On the third day George sent me an email: "I notice that I'm urinating a lot. I feel dehydrated and thirsty. My muscles are sore, and I have a slight headache today. I'm craving sweets again, and I'm hungry most of the time again. The ringing in my ears has come back. I don't sleep well at night and am therefore sleepy in the daytime. I don't have as much energy, and I feel like I've drunk too much coffee. I don't like the way I feel this week. I like the way I felt last week much better."

I had heretofore suspected that the guarana in supplement A had been the most likely cause of George's improvement, but his response to it this week in our trial period did not bear this out. In fact, guarana had made him feel worse.

But another concern surfaced. Because of George's dehydration, frequent urination, his craving for carbohydrates and his battle with obesity, I suspected he might have diabetes. Might diabetes be causing his depression? I had never conducted a scientific study on the topic, but my impression over the years was that depression often precedes diabetes by several years and that depression is more severe in people with diabetes.

I sent an email to George and suggested he have his blood sugar (glucose) tested, I also asked if he had any family history of diabetes.

George replied, "I'll get the blood test for glucose. Yes, obesity and diabetes run in my family. Several of my aunts and uncles on my mother's side had diabetes, as did one relative on my father's side. Several first cousins have diabetes."

When the report came back several days later, the test for blood glucose was within the normal range, which meant that George did not have diabetes. I suspected, as did his family physician, that he had impaired glucose metabolism, also known as glucose intolerance, a pre-diabetic condition in which the movement of blood sugar from the bloodstream into cells is slower than normal, but blood sugar has not begun to backup in the bloodstream and therefore does not show up as abnormal in a blood test.

George asked me a question in an email he sent me at the end of the week: "What was I taking last week that helped me so much?"

Although ideally the identity of any of the six substances given to George should not be revealed until after he had tried each of them, I felt it was his right to know.

I told him it was chromium picolinate.

I consulted Dr. Golden and told him that my patient's depression had returned five days after stopping chromium. Dr. Golden felt my theory that chromium was responsible for the lifting of my patient's depression would be strengthened if a blood test revealed that the patient was deficient in chromium at the time when he was depressed.

I emailed George and asked him if he would go to his family physician and have his blood tested. He did so. A few days later, the laboratory reported that no chromium was detected in George's blood. This confirmed what I was beginning to suspect might be the case: When George felt awful, no chromium was detected in his blood.

Week Four

During week four, George took 100 milligrams of ginseng per day. He reported that he felt better on Monday and Tuesday afternoons than he had felt the week before. He had somewhat more energy and less appetite, but by the fifth day he felt depressed.

In his email report, he wrote, "I feel dehydrated even though I've been drinking a lot of fluids. I run out of energy in the afternoon and evening. Sore muscles, slight headache, and tired."

Week Five

At the beginning of the fifth week, George began taking 50 micrograms of selenium per day.

On the fourth day, he sent me the following email: "I don't have much energy. I don't feel as good as I did a few weeks ago. Not as relaxed. I'm not sleeping well, and I don't wake up rested."

Again, I consulted Dr. Golden. He felt that the evidence was so persuasive that chromium picolinate was the active antidepressant ingredient for George that it would be unethical to continue the trial—tantamount to withholding an effective treatment. Our opinion was that he should resume chromium picolinate on a regular basis and continue taking 125 milligrams of Zoloft per day.

I had planned to make this recommendation to George during our next scheduled meeting six days later, which would be during the sixth week of the trial.

Obviously George was thinking along the same lines, as I received an email from him on Monday of the next week before our next session on Wednesday. His message stated, "I fudged this weekend and took 200 micrograms of chromium picolinate each day. I felt great all weekend, had good energy, and was relaxed. Hope this hasn't hurt the test."

Week Six

On Wednesday of the sixth week, George and I met. He appeared bright and not depressed. His appearance again reminded me of the day he entered my office soon after he had started taking supplement A, and also after taking chromium during the second week of the trial.

I told George I was pleased he had in effect ended the trial by taking chromium. I told him I had consulted with Dr. Golden and we both agreed that he should resume chromium picolinate on a regular basis and continue to take 125 milligrams of Zoloft per day.

George responded, "I want to continue the chromium, but I don't want to take the Zoloft. I think chromium is a better antidepressant for me than Zoloft."

I expressed my apprehension about his discontinuing Zoloft but respected his decision. I thought his depression probably would return within one month, at which time we could decide if he wished to resume taking Zoloft. Meanwhile, I urged him to continue sending me an email every day or two between sessions and to keep me up to date regarding any changes in his health.

That weekend, on a Saturday, George sent me the following email: "I didn't sleep real sound last night, and I had a lot of dreams again, like I did when I first started taking chromium. I think my really vivid dreaming has to do with taking chromium too late in the day. I'm going to take it tomorrow no later than 3:00 P.M. We'll see. I felt very good this morning, cheerful. I feel strong physically and very sharp mentally. It was a great day!"

On Sunday, George reported, "It worked. I took the last dose of chromium earlier in the day and slept well. I have felt great all day. Physically I'm feeling better than I can remember, and I'm feeling just as good mentally. I'm so excited. I hope this continues, as I feel so normal. Chromium is definitely doing something to the way my body is handling food. I'm not craving sweets and I'm not hungry all the time as I used to be, and I don't think about food constantly."

End of Six-Week Trial

The trial was now over—slightly prematurely, as it lasted five weeks instead of six—but it was evident from the information gleaned during the test that a pattern had clearly emerged.

In summary, the main points that surfaced during the trial were as follows:

- George's symptoms had disappeared when he took a chromium-rich "health pill."

- His symptoms had started to return within three days of his discontinuing this pill.

- He had responded to chromium picolinate as a single ingredient in the single-blind trial.

- He had not responded positively to any of the other ingredients in the single-blind trial, which suggested that it was only the chromium picolinate that was the antidepressant agent.

- His symptoms lifted again when he resumed chromium picolinate during the fifth week of the single-blind trial.

- When he had been depressed, no chromium had been detected in his blood.

Another Retesting of George's Chromium Level

After ending the trial in early June, George began taking 200 micrograms of chromium picolinate twice each day, but he decided not to take Zoloft due to the side effects of feeling "slowed down, ears ringing, and sexual impairment." He told me he felt "great" while taking chromium alone, better in fact than when he was taking Zoloft and chromium.

I told Dr. Golden that my patient was feeling great while taking chromium picolinate alone, with no antidepressant. Dr. Golden suggested it would be further evidence of chromium's efficacy if a repeat blood test revealed chromium was present while George was free of depression. I told Dr. Golden I didn't see the point, that it made sense that chromium would be in his blood because he was taking it.

"Not necessarily so," Dr. Golden answered. "Neither you nor I know whether he is absorbing chromium and what amounts must be ingested to get a detectable blood level." I deferred to Dr. Golden's wisdom and agreed and asked George if he was willing, once again, to have his blood tested for chromium. He said it made sense and cheerfully went to his family physician to have his blood tested again for chromium.

The analysis of George's blood seven days after resuming chromium, revealed the presence of chromium, 0.9 micrograms per liter. The normal range is 0.1–2.1 micrograms per liter.

I told George his blood tested positive for chromium while he was taking chromium picolinate and not feeling depressed, and that this was more evidence that chromium was helping him.

On July 7, six weeks after George began taking chromium picolinate regularly without Zoloft, he emailed, "I feel perfect, better than I have felt in a least a decade."

I spoke with him by phone and asked whether he attributed his improvement to chromium or Zoloft.

He answered, "Before Zoloft I had suicidal thoughts and was tired. I wanted to die. With Zoloft I improved some but it made me slow physically. I still saw my life behind me. Now that I have stopped Zoloft and am taking only chromium, I see the life that is ahead of me and I have energy. It's the first time I can remember in a long time being hopeful about the future."

During the weeks and months that followed, I continued to see George weekly and to exchange frequent emails. I also continued to keep detailed notes, almost on a daily basis.

Over the next few months, George took varying amounts of chromium. He observed that when he took less than 400 micrograms per day, his depression, hunger, and tiredness returned. When he felt stressed, he took 1,000 micrograms per day, but at that level he felt "jittery" and his blood level of chromium rose to 2.3 micrograms. We had established a therapeutic window between 400 and 1,000 micrograms per day. Based on his weight, that range was between 2 to 5 micrograms of chromium per pound of body weight for him.

On three or four occasions during the next few months, he stopped taking chromium to see what, if anything, would happen. Each time his depression returned within three or four days, and it then disappeared within twenty-four hours after resuming chromium.

How Does Chromium Help Depression?

My reactions to this discovery puzzled me. The clinical and laboratory evidence was compelling, but I had never observed such a dramatic improvement. I began asking myself the question, "How did chromium accomplish these results?" My best guess was that chromium helped Zoloft increase serotonin in George's brain. I based my very tentative theory on the following: his responses to chromium—the lifting of depression, an increase in dreaming, a decrease in appetite, and increase in energy—were similar to the responses of many patients who take medications that increase brain serotonin, such as Prozac, Zoloft, and Paxil. I assumed that chromium had simply augmented the effects of the SSRI.

George had told me that his daughter, Elizabeth, had the same symptoms he had—depression, craving for sweets, weight gain, and unexplained fatigue—and he wanted me to evaluate her to see if chromium picolinate might help her as much as it had helped him. He had suggested she call me.

CHAPTER 12

Elizabeth:
A Careful Observer

In completing one discovery we never fail to get an imperfect
knowledge of others of which we could have no idea before, so that
we cannot solve one doubt without creating several new ones.

—JOSEPH PRIESTLEY (1733–1804), *prolific English writer and*
experimentalist, best known for his discovery of oxygen

The day after Elizabeth's father asked me to see her, she left a message on my answering machine. She introduced herself as the twenty-three-year-old daughter of George and asked me to call her to arrange an appointment. I returned her call.

She commented, "Dad told me it had taken him almost thirty years to find relief from depression and he wants to spare me that agony and wasted time. He wants to see—and so do I— if chromium will help me as much as it has helped him."

I told Elizabeth I would be happy to see her, but first we had to set a frame. To do that I would have to ask her some questions, which was fine with her. I asked her if she was being treated for depression. She indicated she was seeing a psychologist. I suggested Elizabeth talk over the possibility of our meeting with her psychologist. The next day she called again and said her psychologist thought meeting with me was a good idea. I told Elizabeth I was willing to meet with her, but only for a brief period of time, because she already was in psychotherapy and I was seeing her father. Moreover, I would limit my questions to her depression and not to her personal life. Elizabeth agreed to this frame. We set an appointment for two days later.

Meeting Elizabeth

I greeted Elizabeth in my waiting room and asked her into my office.

She began the interview as follows: "Like I said to you on the phone, Dad told me how much chromium has helped him. I work in the family business with Dad and I see him almost everyday. Dad's a good man, a warm-hearted person, but he can be so irritable and impatient sometimes. I guess that his irritability is his way of showing depression. It's obvious to me and to other people at work that he's been on an even keel lately. He said he wanted me to find out if chromium might help me too."

I told Elizabeth I wanted to understand the biological (for lack of a better word) parts of her difficulties. In other words, I wanted to limit our interaction to a discussion of her symptoms of depression. I didn't want to pry into her personal, psychological life. That was between her and her psychologist. I asked her to describe her symptoms and how long she had been troubled by them.

She explained, "The way I see it is that I've got two big problems: depression and craving sweets. As you can see, I've put on way too many pounds. I've tried to lose weight, but can't. My family doctor told me my cholesterol is way too high, and I really need to lose weight. He suggested Weight Watchers diet and exercise. I tried Weight Watchers, but it didn't work for me. And I've been too tired to exercise. I should be able to control myself, but I can't. I'm disgusted with myself."

"How long have you been struggling with these problems?" I asked.

Elizabeth answered right away: "Constantly since I was thirteen years old. Well, not constantly, but almost all the time. In the past couple of years, my depression and craving for sweets is worse during the week before my [menstrual] period."

I said to Elizabeth, "You, like many people, blame yourself for your problems, but you might have a chemical imbalance that is contributing to your depression. Craving for and eating sweets might be a signal of that imbalance."

She asked how I knew she had a chemical imbalance, and I told her I wasn't certain. It was just a theory. She asked me to explain more and I said to her, "Some researchers think that the type of depression you have, the type that is associated with excessive hunger, is due to low levels of serotonin in your brain, and your craving for and eating sweets may be the way your body is trying to fix the problem.[1–8]

Elizabeth frowned, then asked, "I don't understand. Can you say more?"

I did my best to explain. "Eating sweets causes your pancreas to secrete insulin, which helps tryptophan get into you brain. Tryptophan is the building block that is needed to make the 'feel-good' chemical serotonin in the brain."

Elizabeth agreed, "Eating sweets does make me feel better for a while, for an hour or two, but that's not much a solution because I crash in an hour or two and am hungry all over again. And I gain weight. I know sugar bingeing is bad for me, but I can't seem to help it."

I told her that I was aware of at least one study that showed that overweight people do feel better after consuming carbohydrates.[9] I also agreed with her that eating carbohydrates isn't a good long-term solution. Bingeing on carbohydrates is a little like burning a super-flammable fuel in a race car. It will accelerate fast, but it doesn't last.

Elizabeth asked if I knew of any medications that would help cravings other than Zoloft. I told her I didn't know of any medication that was superior to Zoloft. Unfortunately, I explained, antidepressant medications have side effects.

Elizabeth commented, "How well I know that. My psychologist—I like her a lot—told me three or four years ago that she thought I needed an antidepressant and referred me to a psychiatrist who prescribed Prozac. I can't remember the amount. Maybe 20 milligrams a day? But that made me feel weird. I stopped it and the psychiatrist prescribed Zoloft. I take 50 milligrams a day and it does cut down my cravings somewhat and it helps my mood a little. Do you think chromium will help?"

I didn't know the answer to her question and told her so, but I was willing to conduct a trial identical to that her father had undergone.

Single-Blind Trial

I suggested a plan to Elizabeth that was identical to the plan conducted with her father. I would give her five envelopes. She would not know what any of them contained. Only one envelope would contain chromium. The others would contain ingredients that were safe, but not known to have an impact on depression. She would take one of the pills in the envelope labeled "week #1" each morning from Monday through Friday, and so on for six weeks. At the end of each week, she would fill out the SCL-90 self-rating scale. Elizabeth understood and agreed.

Her responses were almost identical to those of her father. She had no response to vitamin C (500 milligrams per day), guarana (300 milligrams per day), ginseng (100 milligrams per day), or selenium (50 micrograms per day). When chromium picolinate, 300 micrograms per day, was added to her ongoing Zoloft treatment, her depression lifted within three or four days.

Chromium Helps Atypical Depression and PMS

When I saw Elizabeth the next week she expressed pleasure in how much better she had felt during the past week, when unbeknownst to her, she had been taking chromium. Her carving for carbohydrates was less, she had more energy, and her depression had lifted. Furthermore, she did not have her usual symptoms of premenstrual syndrome (PMS). But she was critical of the self-rating scale.

Elizabeth said, "There were no questions pertaining to a woman's menstrual cycle, and everybody knows that a woman's mood, at least mine, fluctuates at that time."

She handed me the self-rating scale she had completed at the end of the week before. In the margins, she had written, "During week #3: Best I have felt. *NO PMS* [Elizabeth's emphasis]."

I admired her keen observation and told her so.

Overlap of Symptoms
Among Atypical Depression and PMS

At first, I was quite puzzled that chromium had helped Elizabeth's PMS and atypical depression. But as I continued to review the topics in the literature, it became apparent to me that atypical depression and PMS share many of the same symptoms—mood swings, carbohydrate craving, a tendency to gain weight, and lethargy. These symptoms in common suggest that atypical depression and PMS have a common biochemical imbalance. Moreover, drugs (SSRIs) that increase the sensitivity of the body to insulin and increase serotonin help both atypical depression and PMS. There is an extensive literature on this topic in medical journals.[10–20]

I considered whether chromium had boosted the effectiveness of Zoloft, and the combination had corrected some underlying chemical imbalance and relieved both PMS and atypical depression. Regardless of how chromium had helped her, we both were certain it had. We agreed that she should continue to take chromium.

Follow-up

Elizabeth returned to her psychotherapist, and I didn't see her again until we met accidentally five years later. I was walking in a shopping mall one day when I heard someone call my name. I looked around and saw a bubbly, cheerful, thin woman. She asked if I knew who she was. I thought she was Elizabeth, but I was unsure. Sensing my hesitation, she said, "I'm Elizabeth. I've lost about forty pounds since I last saw you." She added, "I continue to take chromium, and it has enabled me to adhere to a diet and has given me enough energy to exercise."

I told her how pleased I was to see her. I wish I could have asked her several questions, but the location wasn't right for that. We said goodbye. But that's getting ahead of the story.

CHAPTER 13

Do No Harm

Primum non nocere. First, do no harm.

—ATTRIBUTED TO HIPPOCRATES (460–377 B.C.), *known as the father of medicine*

I was positive that chromium picolinate had helped George's atypical depression, and it had helped his daughter Elizabeth's atypical depression and PMS. Both of them planned to continue taking chromium indefinitely and they asked me if it was safe. I told them I needed to review the literature in-depth to be absolutely certain that chromium is safe before answering their question. The first and foremost concern of all physicians is for safety. *Do no harm.* This concern is embodied in the Hippocratic oath—the oath most medical students take during the ceremony marking their graduation from medical school.

Before giving chromium to George, I had read the chapter on chromium in the authoritative book, *Modern Nutrition in Health and Disease.*[1] This work, published in 1994, is the standard, basic reference work on nutrition used by many physicians, researchers, and nutritional scientists. The author of the chapter on chromium was Forrest H. Nielsen, Ph.D., a research nutritionist, biochemist, and former director of the Grand Forks Human Nutrition Research Center—a large, respected research facility funded by the United States government—that mainly focuses on the role of mineral elements in nutrition.

Dr. Nielsen's book chapter concluded with the following unequivocal statement:

> *Toxicity through oral ingestion of [trivalent chromium, which includes chromium picolinate] is not a practical concern for humans.*

In other words, taking chromium picolinate by mouth is not toxic (dangerous) for human beings.

Based on this authoritative review, I felt justified in recommending chromium picolinate to George and Elizabeth—and to other patients in the future—and that chromium would *do no harm* and might substantially help other patients. However, as persuasive and authoritative as Dr. Nielsen's chapter was, I felt compelled to dig deeper and review all the *original* articles I could find on chromium's safety. In the remainder of this chapter, I will go into my review of the safety literature on chromium in detail. Much of this review occurred after I began giving chromium to other patients.

Basic Facts about Chromium

Chromium exists in many forms. The two most common forms are trivalent chromium and hexavalent chromium. They are as different as chlorine gas is from sodium chloride (table salt). Both contain the element chlorine, but in different chemical states. Chlorine gas is toxic and sodium chloride is used to season food.

Trivalent chromium is safe and is an essential nutrient. It is also known as chromium (III) or nutritional chromium. Trivalent chromium exists naturally in the tissues of all living organisms, including plants and the human body. Chromium *picolinate* is a type of trivalent chromium. Chromium-containing foods include organ meats, mushrooms, broccoli, brewer's yeast, cheese, and wheat germ. However, it is difficult to get enough chromium from eating these foods. Moreover, the typical American diet, which is high in sugar and flour, causes a loss of chromium by excretion of chromium in the urine. The U.S. Department of Agriculture (USDA) estimates that most Americans are chromium deficient.

Trivalent chromium is not to be confused with chromium (VI) or hexavalent chromium. Hexavalent chromium is highly toxic. For instance, even inhalation of dust containing hexavalent chromium is known to cause lung cancer. Chromium VI is a man-made byproduct of industrial processes, including automobile manufacturing and hide tanning. Hexavalent chromium was the type of chromium referred to in the popular movie of recent years titled *Erin Brockovich*.

A Detailed Review of Trivalent Chromium's Safety

I planned to begin my evaluation of chromium's safety by reviewing some of the basic principles of toxicology.

Potential Harm from Ordinary Substances

Toxicologists distinguish between acute toxicity (ill effects from a single dose), chronic toxicity (ill effects over a long time), and benefit/risk ratio.

Acute toxicity. Acute toxicity refers to an adverse health event that results from short-term exposure to a substance. Almost all substances, even those necessary for the proper functioning of the human body, can be harmful, highly toxic, or even lethal if ingested in absurdly large amounts all at once. Table salt (sodium chloride) is necessary for the normal composition of our body fluids. Yet, if a 150-pound person were to eat a cup of salt (about 8 ounces) at one time, that amount would be quite toxic and perhaps even lethal. Aspirin is one of man's most common medicinals, as billions of doses have been taken for arthritis, headache, and other common ailments. Likewise, if a 150-pound person were to take 2 ounces or about 100 adult-size aspirin tablets at one time, that amount would be extremely toxic or fatal.

Some common foods are harmful and potentially cancer-producing if consumed in extremely large amounts. For example, peanut butter contains two parts per billion of a chemical substance called aflatoxin, which is produced by mold on peanuts. At the small concentration found in peanut butter, aflatoxin is harmless. It is practically impossible for any person to eat enough peanut butter to cause aflatoxin death. If, however, aflatoxin is concentrated several thousands of times greater than in peanut butter, it can be fatal.

Ordinary spices can also be lethal in large amounts. For example, if a 150-pound person were to eat 5 ounces (a little more than two cups) of cloves, this amount would be lethal for many people. The same is true for one cup of cinnamon (3-phenyl-2-propenal or cinnamaldehyde).

Chronic toxicity. Chronic toxicity refers to an adverse health effect that results from long-term exposure to a substance. Many substances are not immediately and obviously toxic over the short term, but chronic exposure can be lethal. Examples are liver cancer from inhalation of benzene over several years, lung cancer from inhalation of asbestos and tobacco smoke, "black lung" from inhalation of coal dust, and skin cancer from chronic exposure to sunlight. Usually, the greater the exposure to the dangerous agent, the greater the risk of developing a disease.

Benefit/risk ratio. Researchers evaluate a new drug or treatment by comparing the potential benefits of treatment compared to the degree of risk without treatment. A topical example is a comparison of the health benefits of taking hormone replacement therapy to reduce the risk of osteoporosis versus risk of developing breast cancer. Another example: imagine what would happen to two groups of people with pneumonia—one group untreated with penicillin compared to a group of people treated with penicillin? In the untreated group, there would be much suffering and death. In the treated group, suffering and death would be reduced, but allergic reactions might occur in a few people. Clearly, the benefit of penicillin in a carefully selected group of patients with pneumonia outweighs the risk due to allergic reactions.

Searching for Safety Information about Chromium

After gaining some perspective on acute toxicity, chronic toxicity, and benefit-to-risk ratio, I narrowed my focus to chromium and evaluated it from each of these perspectives.

Evaluation of Chromium's Potential to Cause Acute Toxicity

I asked, "How much trivalent chromium picolinate can a person take on a daily basis without causing harm?" I found a report published in 1990 by the World Health Organization (WHO) based on research conducted in the Netherlands by J.A. Janus and E.I. Krajnc.[2] The study estimated what amount of trivalent chromium could be administered to rats before the level became fatal. Translating from the rat into human terms, the results of the study showed that a 150-pound person would have to take *all at once* the equivalent of 35,000 to 100,000 of the 400-microgram chromium picolinate pills that George and Elizabeth had been taking. The obvious conclusion from this information suggested to me that chromium was very safe.

The researchers concluded that the lethal dose was an oral "LD_{50}" value in the range of 185–615 milligrams per kilogram of body weight. LD_{50} ("LD" stands for "lethal dose") is a standard measure that researchers use to describe short-term toxicity. It represents the amount of a single dose of a substance that results in the death of 50 percent of experimental animals.

The only other reference I could locate concerning short-term toxicity was an article published in 1969 by Henry F. Smyth, M.D., of the American Industrial Hygiene Association. According to Dr. Smyth and his colleagues, the toxic amount of trivalent chromium is more than *one million* times higher than the daily amounts taken by my two patients. Dr. Smyth and his colleagues reported in their study that a single dose of trivalent chromium at 11.26 milligrams per kilogram of body weight is extremely toxic.[3] I was unable to find the original experiments upon which Dr. Smyth based this conclusion. I tried to contact him, but learned that he had died in 1987. I also learned that the American Industrial Hygiene Association had established in his memory the Henry F. Smyth Award, which annually bestows an award to the person who makes an outstanding contribution to environmental safety.

In summary, I gathered from my reading that it is almost impossible to poison laboratory animals with chromium in a single dose. And, by extension, I was therefore convinced that trivalent chromium picolinate was extremely safe for humans if taken in correct amounts.

A caveat to the reader: Of course, it would be extremely unlikely that anyone would attempt to take thousands of chromium pills at one sitting. I hereby warn anyone who would be inclined to self-medicate not to test the limits of these assertions about chromium or any other substances mentioned. This is a dangerous practice for any substance. The amounts are listed for the sake of comparison only, and anything approaching some of the limits mentioned could be quite harmful, as well as fatal.

Evaluation of Chromium's Potential to Cause Chronic Toxicity

Having satisfied myself that chromium is safe in appropriate amounts of single doses taken daily, I wondered, "For what length of time can a person take chromium without doing any harm?"

I found several articles indicating that consumption of chromium over long periods of time is indeed entirely safe.

One article in particular that I found interesting and impressive because of its thoroughness and study design was a report of experiments conducted in 1975 by two German cancer researchers, Drs. Stanislav Ivankovic and Rudolph Preussmann. These investigators fed rats, over their full normal lifespan, the equivalent of 200,000 to 400,000 times more than the daily amounts taken by George and Elizabeth.[4] No adverse effects were observed. Based largely on this experiment, the United States Environmental Protection Agency (EPA) established that a *daily* exposure of 70,000 micrograms of chromium daily over a lifetime does not pose appreciable risk.[5] By inference, that would mean that it would be safe for a 150-pound person to take 175 of the 400 micrograms pills per day for life without suffering damaging side effects.

Does Chromium Have Any Unwanted Effects?

I found one report that chromium picolinate might damage chromosomes, and thus might lead to cancer. This study was done in cell cultures, not in a living organism.

The report was in an article published in 1995 describing an experiment conducted by Diane Stearns, Ph.D., who at that time was working as a fellow in the chemistry department at Dartmouth as an inorganic chemist.[6] Dr. Stearns placed ovarian cells of Chinese hamsters in petri dishes to which she added a mixture of trivalent chromium picolinate, chromium chloride, and picolinic acid. She found that this mixture caused damage to the chromosomes in the ovarian cells, and therefore concluded that chromium picolinate might cause cancer in human beings.

After carefully thinking about this study, I doubted the relevance of the conclusion for two reasons. First, the experiment was not conducted by feeding chromium to living animals. In scientific parlance, it was an *in vitro* or "test-tube" experiment. Results from test-tube experiments cannot be extrapolated to predict results as if similar research had been carried out on living laboratory animals. And secondly, the cells in the petri dishes were treated with very high concentrations of chromium.

The Stearns study seemed weak to me. But since I am not a trained researcher, I wished to get the opinion of an expert.

I began searching for an experienced and respected chromium research scientist to evaluate the Stearns study, and found Dr. Richard Anderson, who received his Ph.D. in biological chemistry in 1973 from Iowa State University, conducted postdoctoral research for the next two years at Harvard Medical School, and in 1976 joined the Human Nutrition Research Center in Beltsville, Maryland. Over the next twenty-one years, he studied the nutritional role of chromium, as well as other trace elements, in human health and disease. He has published 147 articles and numerous book chapters, most of which were about chromium.

The results of Dr. Anderson's evaluation were presented in March 1996 at the Society of Toxicology's annual meeting.[7] He published an article on his evaluation a year later, discussing the Stearns study and concluding that the interpretation of the data from that study was "extremely questionable."

From my reading and review of the medical and scientific literature, and discussion with Dr. Anderson, I was convinced that trivalent chromium does not cause cancer or increase the risk of cancer. In addition, I felt satisfied that individuals face little or no risk of any side effects of any kind if chromium is taken by mouth with the proper dosage.

Note: Not long afterward, an independent advisory panel in the United Kingdom known as the Committee on Mutagenicity (COM) requested duplication of the Stearns study as part of a yearlong, comprehensive, scientific review of chromium picolinate's safety. The replication study, conducted by an independent laboratory, tested chromium picolinate and found no chromosomal damage.[8-9] This finding served to strengthen and affirm my own conclusions.

Benefit/Risk Ratio: Is It Safe NOT to Take Chromium?

As I was reading numerous articles with the question in mind, "Is chromium safe?" I gradually came to realize another equally important question: "Is it safe *not* to take chromium?"

I came upon a large body of information proving the benefits of taking chromium and the dangers of not taking it. That is to say, the benefits of taking chromium far outweigh any theoretical risk.

A deficiency of chromium causes several adverse symptoms in the human body. One of these symptoms is a diabetic-like condition with an elevated blood sugar level and elevated serum insulin, which may lead a person down the treacherous path to type 2 diabetes.[10-11] Another symptom of lack of adequate chromium is a stiffening of the arteries, which is usually the first stage in atherosclerosis (hardening of the arteries).[12-15] And a deficiency of chromium causes an increase in cholesterol.[16]

I also read results of studies of rats and chromium deficiency. While one cannot directly extrapolate results from rats to humans, the conclusions nevertheless confirmed in my mind that a *lack of chromium* may indeed be harmful. One study showed that rats whose diets were chromium-deficient had a shorter life span because of clogging of the aorta, the major artery leading from the heart.[17] Another study showed that chromium deficiency *decreases* the lifespan of rats, while chromium supplementation *increases* the lifespan of rats—increasing it by as much as 25 percent.[18] Still another study using rats as subjects showed that a deficiency of chromium impaired reproductive ability.[19]

Conclusion on Chromium's Safety

In summary, my long and in-depth review of the medical and scientific literature convinced me that chromium picolinate is safe—both immediately as a single dose and after taking it for an extended period, if not taken in amounts that exceed 1,000 micrograms per day. I became convinced that it is far safer to take chromium than not to take it.

In addition—as this book goes to press—there have been more than 2,000 human subjects studied in thirty-five clinical trials. In every one of these trials, not one reported a serious side effect as a result of anyone taking chromium picolinate.

After determining that chromium is safe, I turned my attention to learning how chromium works in the human body. However, I was just beginning that review, when it was interrupted by the near-fatal illness of one of my patients.

CHAPTER 14

Sara: Lost and Wounded

My life closed twice before its close—
It yet remains to see
If Immortality unveil
A third event to me.

—EMILY DICKINSON (1830–1886) *as quoted by Sara*

I had been meeting with Sara since 1984, seven years before George first walked into my office that day in 1991.

First Meeting

I first met Sara in the hospital. She had been admitted because of a second suicide attempt. Her excellent and dedicated psychiatrist at the hospital called to ask if I would evaluate one of his patients and offer a "second opinion on this enigma of a patient." I readily agreed.

Before seeing Sara, her psychiatrist and I sat down and discussed her current and past history. A thick, voluminous chart sat on the table before us. He told me that Sara was in her late twenties and had been under psychiatric care for four years. Two years prior she had made her first suicide attempt. She had been hospitalized several times since then (over the past two years) because of depression and anorexia. During the past week before I was asked to see the patient, she had attempted suicide again.

Sara's current psychiatrist had made a diagnosis of major (severe) depression with atypical features. I asked him to describe her atypical symptoms, and he said "excessive appetite and unexplained tiredness."

Additional diagnoses at various times by various psychiatrists included seasonal affective disorder (SAD or "winter blues" as it is often called), post-traumatic stress disorder, borderline personality disorder with self-mutilation, bipolar II disorder (recurrent depressive episodes alternating with periods of excessive elation), multiple personality disorder, and anorexia nervosa. Different psychiatrists had prescribed numerous anti-depressant and antipsychotic medications with little success.

In spite of all efforts of the hospital staff during this admission, Sara tended to be uncooperative and disruptive as she had during each of her former hospitalizations. In addition, she refused to eat and was dangerously close to death from starvation. She had fired several staff psychiatrists who had been assigned to her, and "now she's about to do the same to me," her psychiatrist said.

As I listened to the problems of this obviously deeply troubled person, I was somewhat apprehensive about meeting her and seeing what I imagined to be a ghastly physical and emotional sight. At the close of the review of Sara's problems and diagnoses, her psychiatrist thanked me for coming and added, with what I intuited were tones of apology, hopelessness, and relief—because he was shifting the burden temporarily from his shoulders to mine—"Good luck."

I went to Sara's hospital room, knocked on the door, and asked if I could come in. I heard a weak, but strident and impatient voice mutter, "Come on in."

I opened the door and saw Sara for the first time. She was lying in bed, hooked up to IVs. She was wasted, with eyes and cheeks sunken. Her hair had not been combed. She picked up a thick pair of glasses and put them on. She sat up and looked angry, and seemed suspicious of my intrusion into her room.

She said, in a confrontational sort of tone, "Who are you? Why are you here?"

I introduced myself and told her that her psychiatrist and the hospital staff had asked me to see her for a second opinion. "They are puzzled by you," I said.

She retorted, "The same list of questions, another diagnosis? Get out! I don't need any more of that crap."

"I'll leave if you insist," I assured her, "but first I would really like to know a little about you as a person—not just to make or confirm a diagnosis. May I sit down?"

With that, Sara shrugged her shoulders, as if exasperated, and reluctantly agreed, "OK. Sit down. Where is your cookbook of questions?"

"What do you mean?" I asked.

She smirked and said, "You know, your list of veterinary questions: How is your appetite, your energy level, whether I get the required eight hours of sleep?"

"I'm here to try to help you, but you're fighting with me already. I wonder why." I added, "As I've already tried to indicate, before asking specific questions, I'd like to know about you—who you are, not just your symptoms, even though they are quite important. And I'd like to know what might be causing your behavior toward the staff, and am wondering what in your past might explain it."

Sara seemed to soften a little and said, "Humm . . . Go ahead."

"Is there anything you have enjoyed in the past?"

Sara seemed to sense my genuine wish to know and answered, "I enjoy reading. I'm a teacher."

She did not volunteer more. I then asked, "Who are your favorite writers?"

Her eyes seemed to brighten and I thought I heard a lilt in her voice as she replied, "Oh, so many. Uh . . . Emily Dickinson, Mark Twain, Thoreau, Edgar Allen Poe."

"You mentioned Dickinson first. Will you to tell me what you like about her," I asked.

"She conveys so much meaning in so few words. Her word pictures are so beautiful and poignant, but so simple."

"Your favorite poem of hers?" I asked. Her voice and expression seemed pensive as she answered, "My Life Closed Twice.'"

"I'm not familiar with it. Will you recite a part of it?"

With a soft and tender voice, she quoted:

> *My life closed twice before its close—*
> *It yet remains to see*
> *If Immortality unveil*
> *A third event to me.*

Unexpectedly, I felt sad. I quickly reminded myself that it's OK to feel her sadness but to keep it in check and use that feeling to further understand her. She looked down, I thought, to avoid possibly feeling disappointed that I might not understand her. As if to acknowledge her sadness and loss, I looked down, too. Why do people bow their heads in grief? We both sat silently, heads bowed, allowing silence to speak. An aura of sadness, of loss, of estrangement seemed to fill the room. I felt if I had spoken, it would have been irreverent, a disturbance of something delicate, sacred. The only sound was the drip, drip, drip of her IV fluids.

After a few moments, I sensed that Sara was looking at me. I looked up and saw that she was. All the light in her eyes had gone. The conspicuously pointed-down corners of her mouth, etched by years of disappointment, brought to my mind the ancient Greek mask of tragedy. I wondered what person, what injuries were hidden behind that mask. After a few more moments of silence—when it did not seem brusque to speak—I asked, "Other authors?"

She answered, "Mark Twain is a favorite— his biting wit, as seen in *Letters from the Earth.* Thoreau inspired me. He was able to live life profoundly but simply, unconventionally. And Hawthorne. He was a product of his time, but he rebelled against prejudice."

Another moment of silence, and then I asked, "You mentioned Poe. What do you recall by him?"

She looked forlorn and said, "'The Raven.'"

"Will you quote a few lines from it?" I asked.

Sara inhaled deeply and I thought I detected resignation in her eyes as she quoted:

> *Lonely yet all undaunted, in this rebuilt land enchanted*
> *In my heart by horror haunted—tell me truly, I implore*
> *Is my love within you? Tell me . . . tell me, I implore . . .*
> *Quoth the raven, sadly, 'Never . . . .more?'*

Why was she so sad and lost? Who had failed to accept her love? Had she lost a loved one during childhood? Her psychiatrist had told me that both of her parents and her older brothers and sisters were alive. There had been no obvious childhood losses. Looking for answers to this question, I asked her, "May I change direction and ask you a question about your past?" She said yes.

"The poems you quote sound so sorrowful," I said. "I wonder if you lost someone whom you loved—someone who loved you?"

With that question, she took off her glasses, appeared on the verge of tears, and answered. "Please leave," she said as if running from sadness. Then she changed her mind. "No, stay." And after hesitating a few moments, she said with obvious anguish, "My aunt, my mother, died."

I waited for clarification, but Sara remained silent. After a few moments, I said, "I'm confused. Your aunt or your mother died?"

She explained, "My aunt. My parents had several girls before me, and I don't think they wanted another one. My aunt and uncle wanted a child, but they couldn't get pregnant, so I was sent to live with them. They adopted me. After they adopted me, my aunt got pregnant and died during childbirth."

To make certain I had understood her, I repeated what she had told me, which she confirmed. Then I asked, "How old were you when she died?"

"Four. Almost four and a half. I went back to live with my parents."

"How did you get along with your aunt? Can you tell me a little about her?"

I thought I saw a glow of warmth in Sara's eyes as she said, "She was wonderful. She loved me. She read to me and taught me how to read by the time I was four. I loved it. I loved *her*."

Sara reached into her purse, pulled out a ring, showed it to me, and explained, "She gave me this ring. I wore it for a couple of years, until my fingers got too large. Now I carry it with me in my purse, always."

After a few moments of silence, I asked her, "Is it possible that you're starving yourself, trying to get as small as you were at age four, so that the ring will fit your finger again? A symbolic reunion with your aunt?" I thought I saw tears well up, but then Sara seemed agitated, grimaced, retched, and reached for the wastebasket.

After wiping her mouth and hands with a tissue, she replied, "I've had the wish that I was a little girl so someone would take care of me, but I didn't make the connection between that wish and starvation until just now, when you mentioned it. Your question reminds me when, after my aunt's death, each day around dusk, I'd go to the road and look down it, waiting for her to come home. She never did. Guess I didn't understand that she was really gone."

To some degree and for a moment, her loneliness seemed soothed by the closeness we had achieved through understanding. After a moment of consolation, of rest, I asked, "What was it like when you went back to live with your parents?"

Sara grimaced and said, "Awful. Mom didn't want me to begin with—another girl. When I went back to live with her, I had temper tantrums. To try to stop me from having them, she threw cold water in my face. I was a bother to her."

"Your father?" I asked.

Sara responded, "Dad was always gone. Always busy. Even if he'd been at home, I don't think he was cut out to be a parent. Was too self-absorbed."

"Were you close with anyone after your aunt's death?" I asked. "Was there anyone to comfort you?"

Sara answered, "I spent a lot of time playing with my dogs, and cuddling with them. I trusted them. They taught me a lot. There were times when I didn't know whether sights and sounds were real or imaginary and by looking at my dogs' nose and ears, I could determine what was real. And I read a lot and always have. That's why I chose the profession I'm in."

By this time I suspected many of Sara's problems could be traced back to the loss of her aunt-mother; that is, to unresolved grief. I had known several patients who had lost a loved one during childhood and who were unable to watch sad movies, such as *Old Yeller* and *Bambi*. Children's books and movies took them back so painfully close to the actual time of loss that they were unable to read the books or watch the movies. I felt it would have been too direct and potentially wounding to ask Sara if she was bothered by looking at any specific books or movies, so I asked, indirectly, "Are there any children's books that make you too sad to read?"

"Yes. There are also movies I can't watch, can't talk about."

After a few moments, I asked, "What are they?"

She seemed annoyed by my question and scolded me, "You asked if I could talk about them. I told you I couldn't and now you ask if I can."

I felt appropriately admonished and apologized for my clumsiness. She accepted my apology.

Now I was positive I was able to add another to Sara's long list of diagnoses that were forming in my mind: the diagnosis of unresolved grief due to childhood loss.

Treatment Recommendation

Although I had learned something about Sara's anguish, I didn't know what treatment to recommend. Could she be helped? Her wounds were deep and her scars as obvious as those from an extensive, third-degree burn. Would talking about her sorrows and traumas be akin to taking a shell-shocked soldier back to the battlefield? Was the treatment worse than the illness? Was she like a terminally ill patient who desperately needs an operation, but is too ill to survive surgery? Would emotional surgery hasten her death?

Deciding on psychotherapy is not just about answering the one-sided question, "Can the patient tolerate psychotherapy?" It is also about answering the question, "Can the psychoanalyst tolerate the patient's suffering without sinking?" Intensive psychotherapy is a two-person process in which the analyst experiences the patient's feelings, to a controlled extent, and uses these feelings to establish closeness through understanding. And hopefully in the process conveying to the patient, "You're not alone." There is a danger that the analyst might experience pain almost as deeply as the patient. It's a most delicate balance between stepping into the patient's world in search of understanding, then stepping back out of it and conveying that understanding to the patient.

I was certain that entering into analytic psychotherapy with Sara would be a test of an analyst's ability to feel deep pain without being engulfed by it. Sara and the analyst would have to travel together, in memory, to meet people who had unwittingly or worse, perhaps intentionally, almost destroyed her. Sara had barely survived. With the help of an analytic companion, would she be able to go back in time and confront her assailants? Would she be strengthened by the process? Clearly the answers to these questions involved Sara's life or death. I would have to mull them over before making a treatment recommendation to her psychiatrist.

Toward the end of our meeting, I asked Sara if she had any questions. "Yes," she said. "May I speak with you again?"

I was surprised and didn't know how to answer her. I told her that both she and I would need to discuss that with her psychiatrist. The next day, he contacted me and told me Sara wanted me to be her doctor. With some hesitancy, I agreed. Sara and I would meet again and again, for many times over many years.

CHAPTER 15

Giving Sorrow Words

Give sorrow words. The grief that does not speak,
knits up the o'er wrought heart and bids it break.

—WILLIAM SHAKESPEARE (1564–1616)

I came to know Sara as a person as delicate as a recently freed butterfly—and about as ill-prepared to face harsh Nature.

Sara During Her Teens and Twenties

After Sara was sent back to live with her mother, this once placid child was "impossible to manage." She had frequent temper tantrums and her mother either threw cold water on her or beat her. Eager to get some rest, her mother occasionally sent Sara to visit her uncle, the husband of the deceased aunt. Although Sara was never certain, she thinks he sexually abused her.

During Sara's preteen years, she developed eating difficulties. Her appetite became ravenous and almost impossible to control.

She said, "There must be something genetic in my craving for sweets. People on both sides of my family crave sweets. Once I saw one of my uncles eat a gallon of ice cream at one sitting."

"Did you mean to say a pint or a quart of ice cream?" I asked Sara.

Her answer was emphatic. "I realize it's almost unbelievable, but he did eat a gallon of ice cream in less than an hour. Needless to say, they are overweight, and several aunts and uncles on my father's side have diabetes. And my father's mother had diabetes, too. I was afraid of becoming obese like they were, so I refused to eat and became emaciated. My mother scolded me when I refused to eat and would not allow me to leave the table until my plate was clean. When she wasn't looking, I would give food to my dog."

She continued to waste away. But starvation had its rewards for Sara: at least it erased her appetite. When she was taken to see her family doctor because of a urinary tract infection, the physician noticed she was dangerously underweight and hospitalized her. He asked Sara if she was worried or upset about something. She desperately wanted to tell him how sad and lonely she was, but she didn't dare, fearing that her mother would beat her if she told the truth.

To escape her painful family situation, Sara ran away from home at age sixteen and joined a cult. She was "brainwashed." Total subservience to the cult leader was demanded. He regularly had sex with her. During such rapes, she protected herself by picturing herself as another person, with Sara being far away and safe. She summoned imaginary "tough guys," whom she directed to attack the cult leader. Sara developed several more personalities to cope with various types of overwhelming situations. She lost segments of time and was unaware where she had been and what she had done. In other words, Sara developed multiple personality disorder. In fact, she escaped the abusive cult situation by running away in a fugue state, a condition of high anxiety in which a person is barely able to recognize surroundings. She "came to" in the emergency room of another city.

After escaping the cult, Sara worked as a maid for a teacher, who eventually became her emotional aunt-mother and teacher. Right away she saw Sara's gifts for language. She encouraged Sara, and helped her return to school where Sara proved to be an exceptional student and, eventually, a college teacher.

By the time Sara had reached her early twenties, her anorexia gave way to eating binges and she gained weight—up to 200 pounds at one time. On occasion she would go into a trance-like state, buy a dozen doughnuts, and "wolf them down." Sometimes she ate an entire cake at one sitting. When she came to her senses and realized how much she had consumed, she hated herself and induced vomiting and took laxatives. In an attempt to control her eating, she punished herself by taping pictures of ultra-thin models to her bathroom mirror and comparing herself with them. They looked so thin and lovable to her. Sara felt so large, so ugly, so unlovable.

By her mid-twenties, Sara was suffering from severe depression. Various sights, sounds, smells, and personal interactions reminded her of the physical and sexual abuse she had endured. To escape, she would lock herself in a closet and remain there for a day or two, without food or water. She was loved by her students, but her frequent absences from the classroom drew the attention of college administrators. They strongly suggested she get "professional help," which she did, but it was not successful. Eventually she lost her teaching job. This triggered her first suicide attempt. She was hospitalized for a few weeks and discharged. She was readmitted several times due to cutting her arms and burning herself. Later she made another near-fatal suicide attempt and was again hospitalized. It was during that time that I first met her.

Medications Added to Psychotherapy

For Sara, intensive, psychoanalytic psychotherapy was the foundation of her treatment with me. Eventually she grew to trust me, and we worked on issues of trust of others, sadness that she could never make her mother happy, rage with her mother, grief about the loss of her aunt, and rage toward the men who had abused her. Rather than return to the classroom, she decided to tutor selected students, to do volunteer work, and to write.

As helpful as psychotherapy was, it was apparent to both of us that Sara needed more. Her moods fluctuated often, ranging from deep despair to inappropriate elation. I prescribed lithium, which helped stabilize her mood. She was also bothered by obsessive compulsive disorder (OCD). Most of us occasionally have experienced a song that "gets on our mind" and annoys us for a few minutes to a few hours. But for Sara, a song or a thought would "get on her mind" and pester her for hours or days. She also had compulsive rituals, such as taking three-hour-long showers. For this I prescribed several medications. After much trial and error, we found that Paxil was the best drug available for controlling her OCD and her depression. While taking lithium (300 milligrams) three times a day and Paxil (50 milligrams) once a day, Sara was able to function much better in her daily life.

Another of her serious problems, which had bothered her since she was in her late teens, was severe PMS. Each month, during the week before her menstrual periods, Sara's depression, exhaustion, irritability, ravenous hunger, and rage outbursts intensified. Her menstrual cramps were so painful that she was unable to function for two to three days each month. She hated herself for being a woman, and felt she was doomed to suffer each month. The large daily doses of Paxil reduced the severity of her PMS symptoms by "about 50 percent," but her periods continued to be a severe and dreaded problem.

In 1992, Sara developed a bout of severe diarrhea and vomiting that lasted for six weeks. She was unable to take her medications, and her depression returned with a vengeance. She lost weight, loathed herself, was unable to sleep, and felt suicide was the only answer. Her obsessive-compulsive symptoms (repeated hand washing, lengthy showers, repeating phrases over and over) returned and occupied much of her time, essentially incapacitating her. Had she not been in psychotherapy, I am convinced—as was Sara—that she would have committed suicide.

I referred her to a family physician for evaluation. He suspected she had an intestinal parasitic infection but was unable to make a definite diagnosis of her problem. He gave her various medications that finally controlled her vomiting and diarrhea. Sara was then able to resume Paxil and lithium, but they were not as effective as before. She was barely able to perform even the minimal activities of taking care of herself, such as taking a bath or eating.

Sara and I decided to increase Paxil to 60 milligrams a day, a somewhat higher dosage than recommended by the *Physician's Desk Reference* (PDR), but her condition improved only slightly. She was desperate. She had to assist one of her students in a presentation and the deadline was rapidly approaching. It was the result of years of work by Sara and the student. The consequences of failing to make the deadline would be financially disastrous, personally humiliating, and would be a major disappointment to one of the students she tutored.

Trying Chromium

I so wanted to relieve Sara's suffering but felt I had exhausted all the outpatient treatment possibilities of which I was aware. At this point, psychotherapy, lithium, and Paxil were not enough. Another hospitalization seemed inevitable. I suggested this to Sara, but she rejected this option.

What more could I do for her? Might chromium help? I doubted it. I thought chromium had helped George and Elizabeth because they were father and daughter and probably shared some rare genetic disorder. But—driven more by desperation than by hope—I told Sara that I had two patients (in other words, George and Elizabeth) who had benefited from the addition of chromium to their antidepressants.

Sara remembered taking chromium years earlier for appetite suppression and weight control, but she did not remember the dosage. She wanted to try it again and asked how much and what brand to take. I suggested she take 400 micrograms per day of chromium picolinate.

Amazingly, Sara's mood began to lift within three to four days.

She reported, "Dr. McLeod, chromium must be boosting the Paxil. My depression and OCD are less of a problem. My appetite has been curbed and I have more energy. Chromium didn't have these effects when I took it years ago to try to lose weight. Maybe I didn't take a high enough dosage then."

You could have knocked me over with a feather. Another person with depression had responded to chromium.

Chromium's Effect on Premenstrual Syndrome

Two weeks later my astonishment intensified, as Sara told me, "The strangest thing happened. My period started without any warning. And my depression didn't get worse as it usually does before my period. The cramps didn't happen. This was the easiest period in a decade."

"This may be due to the Paxil you're taking," I said.

Sara was obviously annoyed by my statement and objected, "No. That doesn't make sense! As we both know, I've been taking antidepressants (Paxil, Zoloft, Pamelor, and Elavil) for years, and they were only mildly to moderately helpful in relieving my PMS. They decreased my PMS symptoms by about 50 percent, but they never eliminated it. I'm almost positive the benefit is due to chromium."

During several weeks that followed, Sara experimented by taking 400 micrograms of chromium picolinate some weeks and not others. Without it, invariably her excessive appetite, depression, OCD, and premenstrual symptoms worsened. While she was taking chromium, she felt greatly improved. I asked her to specify which symptoms of PMS did and did not respond to the addition of chromium.

She replied, "Chromium eliminates my irritability, depression, hypersensitivity to light and noise, craving for sweets, cramps, and I'm able to work and be around people. Chromium does not help at all with breast swelling and tenderness."

This was one of the most dramatic observations I had ever made during years of practice. That is not to say, however, that chromium relieved all of Sara's symptoms or problems. It did not. She continued to carry remnants of many of her old scars, but they were modified. She learned what they were and could look out for them. They were ameliorated. But Sara's depression was markedly improved, her appetite was under control, her weight returned to normal, and she *never* had another bout of PMS.

Termination of Therapy with Sara

The therapeutic journey with Sara was long and every bit as painful as I had anticipated. It was also even more successful than I had anticipated given the severity of her problems.

During the early months of our work, I was often concerned that she would commit suicide. On several occasions she entered fugue states, drove to some distant city, and "came to" in a hospital or jail. During such absences, I worried that she had committed suicide. Eventually, a combination of treatments—modified psychoanalysis, psychiatric medications, exercise, a low-carbohydrate diet, and chromium—proved to be marvelously uplifting.

Sara and I both decided, after much deliberation, that she had made as much progress as was possible for her. As she phrased it, "From where I've come, this is about as far as I can go." We set a termination date for six months later. During that time, as is often the case, some of her original symptoms returned. She cried and cursed. "You want to get rid of me so you can start seeing a fancy male patient." By this time, Sara was capable of doing her own analytic work. She realized she was experiencing me (transference) as if I was her mother who did get rid of her. During the month before our work ended, Sara became calm and peaceful. She looked back over our years of work together and marveled at her progress. She was so grateful for what we had accomplished.

As Sara and I were ending our last session, she came over and shook my hand. With composure, she said, "Thank you and goodbye." As she walked to the door to leave, I said to her, "Good luck" and was about to say "Goodbye," but the word stuck in my throat as I visualized that little four-year-old girl—looking down that long, dark, lonesome road waiting for her aunt to return.

My intense feeling of sadness as Sara and I were saying farewell helped me understand the extent to which I had been walking in her shoes and carrying her burden of loneliness. I will never forget Sara and her heroic struggles, but realizing I had been walking in her shoes and helping her carry her burdens helped me step out of her shoes and move on, too. Last of all, there was a great deal more I needed to learn about chromium.

PART THREE

From Observation to Explanation

CHAPTER 16

A Prepared Mind: Discovering Chromium's Essential Role in Glucose Metabolism

> *In the fields of observation,*
> *chance favors only the mind that is prepared.*
>
> —LOUIS PASTEUR (1822–1895), *French chemist and bacteriologist*

Sara's response to chromium suggested that the responses of George and Elizabeth had not been a fluke based on their obvious genetic similarity because they were father and daughter. I wondered if chromium might help some of my other depressed patients who were dissatisfied with their responses to antidepressant medications. But what type of depression might it help? To answer this question, I asked myself if George, Elizabeth, and Sara had any symptoms, other than depression, in common. The answer was "yes." George, Elizabeth, and Sara had constant hunger, a tendency to put on excess weight, and a family history of type 2 diabetes. To answer how chromium had helped them, I needed to learn who discovered chromium is an essential nutrient, how was that discovery made, and how does chromium work in the human body.

I was off to the library again.

Discovering Chromium's Role in Glucose Metabolism and Insulin Functioning

It was known in the 1940s that chromium, besides its existence in the earth's soil, was also present in small amounts in plants and animals. In the 1950s and 1960s, scientists discovered that chromium played a necessary role in the metabolism of glucose in rats.[1–5] And, in the latter part of the 1970s, chromium's role as an essential nutrient necessary for insulin to

89

function normally in the human body was proved by a physician whose keen observations will remind us that good luck favors a prepared mind.

Dr. Jeejeebhoy and His Patient: Chromium as an Essential Nutrient

An essential nutrient is a substance that is necessary for the body to function normally, but which the body cannot make itself and therefore must be acquired from the diet. The physician who discovered that chromium is an essential nutrient in man was Dr. Khursheed Jeejeebhoy, professor of gastroenterology at the Toronto General Hospital in Canada. One of his patients was a woman who had developed a blood clot in the main artery that led to her intestines.[6] As a result of the clot, the patient's intestines died and had to be surgically removed to save her life. Thereafter the woman was unable to take food and water by mouth, and had to be fed through her veins—a technique known as total parenteral nutrition (TPN). At that time, nutritionists believed that the TPN mixture contained all essential nutrients. But soon Dr. Jeejeebhoy was to learn that the mixture was incomplete.

After doing well for several months on TPN, the woman's ability to "burn" or metabolize glucose became impaired with the following results: her blood sugar rose to abnormally high levels, her legs tingled, she lost sensation in her legs (peripheral sensory neuropathy), her gait became unsteady (ataxia), and she lost her sense of well-being. Studies showed that the nerves in her legs were not conducting impulses normally. Dr. Jeejeebhoy thought his patient was not producing enough insulin to "burn" blood sugar. Accordingly, he prescribed 50 units of insulin per day, and added it to the TPN mixture. To his surprise, her ability to "burn" glucose did not improve. In other words, the patient's problem was not a deficiency of insulin, but rather her body was not responding normally to insulin.

Dr. Jeejeebhoy suspected that the patient's lack of response to insulin might be due to an absence of chromium in the TPN mixture. He tested his patient's hair and blood for the level of chromium. The results showed that his patient had no detectable chromium in her body. Dr. Jeejeebhoy then added 200 micrograms of chromium (as chromium chloride) per day to the TPN mixture. After only three weeks, his patient's blood glucose returned to normal levels and adding insulin to the TPN mixture was no longer necessary. What was also surprising was that, in spite of the woman's drastically altered bodily state and quite understandable consternation about her condition, her sense of well-being returned.

Dr. Jeejeebhoy described these findings in an article that was published in 1977. I read and re-read this article many times while at the same time reading other articles to try to understand how chromium works in the human body. I found it to be an interesting medical detective story. I mailed my understanding of his case report, as described above, to Dr. Jeejeebhoy and asked him to verify that I had understood the facts of the article correctly. He wrote in reply, "You have indeed reported the case accurately. Chromium restored the patient's sensitivity to insulin."

I soon telephoned Dr. Jeejeebhoy and asked what made him suspect that it was chromium that was missing from the TPN mixture. He replied that he was aware of research conducted some years earlier at the National Institutes of Health (NIH) by Dr. Walter Mertz and colleagues that demonstrated chromium is necessary for the proper functioning of insulin in rats. Dr. Jeejeebhoy was also aware of studies in humans that showed chromium improved the metabolism of glucose in malnourished children and in the elderly.[7–9]

Dr. Freund: Confirmation of Chromium as an Essential Nutrient

I read another article, published two years after Dr. Jeejeebhoy's article, which confirmed the finding that chromium is necessary for insulin to act normally and to metabolism or "burn" glucose. The article was written by Herbert Freund, M.D., who at the time was a surgeon at the Massachusetts General Hospital in Boston.[10]

Dr. Freund had a forty-five-year-old woman patient whose intestines also of necessity had to be surgically removed to save her life. The patient had been fed a TPN mixture intravenously for five months, after which time she then became confused (encephalopathy) and developed an extremely high blood sugar level. Because of her high blood sugar, insulin was added to the TPN mixture. But the addition of insulin to the TPN mixture failed to bring the patient's blood sugar down.

Dr. Freund and his colleagues suspected that the patient's blood sugar was elevated due to an obscure infection and that excessive stress was responsible for her failure to respond to insulin. But extensive diagnostic work-ups, including laboratory tests, failed to find the cause of the woman's elevated blood sugar and confusion. The physicians were puzzled.

At about that time, Dr. Jeejeebhoy's article was published. It caught the attention of Dr. Freund. As a result, Dr. Freund added chromium to his patient's TPN mixture. The woman's response was dramatic. Within *only three days,* her confusion disappeared "completely." Amazingly, her blood glucose level dropped toward the normal range, and she no longer needed insulin in her intravenous mixture.

The observations of Drs. Jeejeebhoy and Freund were repeated and confirmed by other medical scientists.[11–12] Thereafter, chromium was regularly added to TPN solutions, and chromium was recognized as an essential nutrient for the normal metabolism of carbohydrates.[13–14]

Chromium Deficiency and Impaired Functioning of the Brain and Nerves

In both the case reports of Dr. Jeejeebhoy and Dr. Freund, there was evidence that chromium is necessary for the normal functioning of the nervous system. Dr. Jeejeebhoy reported that chromium deficiency damaged nerves in the legs and interfered with their ability to conduct impulses to allow the patient to walk normally. Supplementation with chromium reversed her nerve damage. I wondered if Dr. Jeejeebhoy's patient had been depressed. So I wrote to Dr. Jeejeebhoy with this question, "By 'loss of a sense of well-being,' did you mean your patient was depressed?" Dr. Jeejeebhoy wrote back that she did not have any signs of deep depression. Dr. Freund reported that a deficiency of chromium interfered with normal functioning of the brain and caused confusion in his patient, and when chromium was added her confusion cleared.

I began to wonder if chromium deficiency might interfere with the brain's ability to use glucose, and this might be the *cause* of my patients' depression. How could I determine if George, Elizabeth, and Sara's insulin functioning was abnormal? To answer these questions, I needed to learn more about abnormal functioning of insulin and glucose metabolism.

CHAPTER 17

A Lock and a Key: Normal and Abnormal Glucose Metabolism

The most beautiful thing we can experience is the mysterious.
It is the source of all true art and science.

—ALBERT EINSTEIN (1879–1955), *German-American physicist*

By now I had learned two facts. First, I was positive that chromium had lifted George, Elizabeth, and Sara's depression and it had curbed their craving for carbohydrates and given them more energy. Secondly, I had learned from the work of Dr. Jeejeebhoy and others that chromium is necessary for insulin to function normally. I put these two facts together and came up with the following theory:

Resistance of the body to the action of insulin (insulin resistance)
causes the type of depression that is associated with excessive
appetite and unexplained exhaustion. Chromium helps this type
of depression by restoring the sensitivity of the body to insulin,
which in some unknown way lifts mood, curbs carbohydrate
craving, and overcomes fatigue.

But how did chromium and insulin working together exert these effects on a cellular level?

I knew that trying to explain my observations on a cellular level would take me into the dark realms of endocrinology, metabolism, cellular biology, biochemistry of the brain, and nutrition. To say that I was rusty in these areas is an understatement. I had not studied these fields since my medical school days more than thirty years prior. Moreover, scientists had made huge advances in these fields since my student days. I felt about as ill-prepared for this task as I would exploring a mammoth cave with a tiny flashlight.

But determined to take this journey I was.

What I anticipated as an onerous chore turned out to be endlessly fascinating to me. After reading thousands of scientific articles, reflecting on the symptom patterns of the patients who responded to chromium, cogitating at length, and discussing these topics with several colleagues, at last I came to some understanding of how chromium helps people with atypical depression.

Normal Functioning of Insulin

My first step in this long journey was to understand more about the basic, normal functions of insulin, insulin receptors, glucose metabolism, and chromium in the human body.

Insulin is a hormone produced by the pancreas that helps glucose enter cells.

Insulin sensitive receptors are located on the surface of cells throughout the body. They act as "gates" that must open for glucose to enter the cells. Chromium "lubricates" the locks on the cell gates, thus allowing insulin to open the cell gates and allowing glucose to enter cells, where it is burned to produce energy.

To sustain life, the human body must continuously make energy. Glucose—or blood sugar as it is commonly known—is one of the main sources of fuel for the body, and it is the *only* source of fuel normally used by the brain. We get glucose from the food we eat. Before being converted into energy, glucose must travel from the intestines to cells throughout the body, and then it must enter the cells where it is converted into energy. For this process to occur, there must be cooperation among insulin in the bloodstream, insulin receptors on the surface of cells, and chromium.

Insulin circulates through the bloodstream to various parts of the body looking for its mates—the insulin sensitive receptors. Under normal conditions, when insulin and the insulin receptors meet each other, it's love at first sight. They were made for each other. Insulin fits into insulin receptors, as a key into a lock, and causes the "gates" of the cell to open wide, which allows glucose (and other nutrients) to enter the cells. After a series of steps, the energy stored in glucose is released.

This process of unlocking gates occurs in almost all cells throughout the body—in muscle cells, fat cells, the liver, heart, white blood cells, platelets, eyes, and in the brain—and provides the energy necessary for many purposes. We use this energy to keep our bodies warm, exercise our muscles, make antibodies, repair and replace tissues, and accelerate chemical reactions.

Having understood more about the normal functioning of insulin, I now needed to learn about abnormal functioning of insulin. In other words, what can go wrong?

Malfunctioning of Insulin: Insulin Resistance

In some people, the gates to muscle and fat cells become "rusty" and difficult to open. The cell gates rebuff the action of insulin. The shorthand designation for this condition is insulin resistance. The rusty gates slow the movement of glucose into the cells, which causes an energy shortage, a condition known as impaired glucose metabolism. The pancreas tries to force the cell gates to open by producing more and more insulin, a condition known as hyperinsulinemia. What was once an easy, felicitous engagement between insulin and insulin receptors becomes a struggle that damages organs throughout the body. A deficiency of chromium may play a role in insulin resistance since chromium is an insulin cofactor.

Impaired glucose metabolism and the resultant high levels of insulin damage the body in a number of ways.[1–2]

- **Trunkal obesity (weight centered around the waist).** Insulin stimulates the liver to store excess carbohydrates as fat, especially around the waist. Although excess weight probably is not the primary cause of insulin resistance, it certainly makes it worse. Losing weight reduces insulin resistance.

- **High blood pressure (higher than 130 over 85).** Too much insulin stimulates the kidneys to retain too much salt and fluid, which leads to high blood pressure and increases the risk of having a stroke. In fact, half of people with high blood pressure have insulin resistance![3]

- **Low HDL ("good") cholesterol (below 35 in women and below 40 in men).** Too much insulin causes the liver to use a part of HDL cholesterol to make triglycerides (see following). HDL cholesterol cleans plaque from arteries and lessens a person's risk of heart attack and stroke. Low levels of good cholesterol are associated with an increase in the risk of heart attack and stroke.

- **High triglycerides (above 150).** Too much insulin stimulates the liver to make triglyceride ("bad") blood fat. Triglycerides are the chemical form in which most fat exists in the body. Triglycerides clog arteries and have been linked to heart disease. Eighty-five percent of obese people who have a ratio of triglyceride to HDL cholesterol of 3 or more have insulin resistance.[4] For example, a triglyceride level of 150 and a HDL level of 50 is a ratio of 3.

- **High blood sugar (above 100).** In some people the pancreas gets exhausted from working overtime and trying to force the gates on muscle and fat cells to open to let glucose in. It cannot keep up with the demand for large amounts of insulin for this task. Blood sugar begins to back up in the bloodstream. This early phase of impaired glucose metabolism (when blood sugar is between 100 to 110) is known as glucose intolerance and/or pre-diabetes. As blood sugar levels become higher, a person is said to have type 2 diabetes.

These changes in the body that result from too much insulin increase the risk of having type 2 diabetes, heart attack, and stroke in men and women, and infertility in women due to polycystic ovarian syndrome. (This condition occurs because high levels of insulin force the ovaries to produce too much of the male hormone, which prevents eggs from escaping from the ovary; rather the eggs are retained and form ovarian cysts.) I was beginning to wonder if the type of depression associated with weight gain, excessive appetite, and unexplained exhaustion might be another sign of insulin resistance.

Did Insulin Resistance Cause George, Elizabeth, and Sara's Atypical Depression?

As I was learning about the signs of insulin resistance and the impairment of glucose metabolism it causes, it gradually dawned on me that George, Elizabeth, and Sara had some of the objective or measurable signs of insulin resistance.

Both George and Elizabeth were overweight, with much of their weight centered around their waists. As George phrased it, "I carry a spare tire around my middle." Although Sara was almost emaciated when I met her, she had once weighed as much as 200 pounds. When asked about her weight distribution when she was overweight, she replied, "I looked like I was pregnant," referring to her tendency to put on weight around her abdomen.

Elizabeth's family physician had warned her that her total cholesterol and triglycerides were "seriously elevated," and her HDL ("good") cholesterol was low. He had encouraged her to exercise and lose weight.

All three of my patients had a family history that put them at risk of developing insulin resistance. George had several aunts and an uncle on his mother's side of the family who had "diabetes that came on late in life," that is, type 2 diabetes. By extension, since Elizabeth was his daughter, she was also at increased risk of developing insulin resistance. Sara's biological mother had high blood pressure, and several aunts and uncles on her father's side had type 2 diabetes.

Carbohydrate Craving and Insulin Resistance

But what might cause an excessive appetite, especially for carbohydrates, in insulin resistance? I knew that obesity is often associated with insulin resistance and common sense suggests that excessive appetite precedes obesity. But why specifically did my patients crave sweets and starchy carbohydrates?

When glucose metabolism is impaired, insufficient glucose gets into cells. Sweets and starchy carbohydrates are absorbed rapidly from the intestines. They are a quick fix that sets off a series of steps. First, after eating a large carbohydrate meal, blood sugar levels rise rapidly. The pancreas tries to deal with this load by secreting large amounts of insulin. In most people, the large amount of insulin is able to force open the gates on muscle and fat cells, which allows glucose to enter. But this quick-fix solution backfires, as the excess insulin causes blood sugar levels to fall too low, with the result that the person has an almost desperate hunger for sweets. Moreover, the excess carbohydrates are stored as fat, which worsens insulin resistance.

Attempts to overcome insulin resistance by eating carbohydrates is a little like having a car that is sputtering because clogged fuel lines slow the movement of gas into the cylinders. Temporarily you can overcome the problem by pressing down on the accelerator (secreting more insulin) and forcing more gas through the fuel lines, but this increases pressure in the lines and leads to further narrowing of the fuel lines. One problem will lead to another until the red warning light on the dashboard flashes on, indicating "engine overheating."

Theory Going Forward

Because my patients' depression had responded to chromium—an insulin-sensitizing agent—I suspected that their depression, excessive appetite, and unexplained exhaustion might be due to the insensitivity of their bodies to the action of insulin, that is, to insulin resistance. I knew the "standard" objective signs of insulin resistance: weight gain and/or obesity, low HDL ("good") cholesterol, high triglyceride ("bad" blood fat), high blood pressure, and elevated blood sugar. I was beginning to wonder if their depression and craving for carbohydrates also were signs of insulin resistance. My theory that insulin resistance causes atypical depression was very tentative, and supposed a connection between impaired glucose metabolism and depression. Was there any evidence in the literature to support this? I was off to the library again.

CHAPTER 18

Sadness and Long Sorrow: The Connection Between Impaired Glucose Metabolism and Depression

[There is a] striking relationship between the concentration of glucose in the blood and the normal functioning of the nervous system.
—J.J.R. MacLeod (1876–1935), *Canadian physiologist and co-discoverer of insulin*

For many years I had the impression that impaired glucose metabolism causes depression in some people, especially in those who crave sweets and starchy carbohydrates and who have unexplained exhaustion. Moreover, I had the impression that depression often is an early sign of diabetes.

Several young adults consulted me in the 1970s and '80s for depression, and years later they developed type 2 diabetes. I also noted that their depression seemed more severe and likely to recur compared to other depressed patients. The association between depression and diabetes is illustrated by my encounters with a friend of mine.

Several years ago Al called me and said he was very depressed. He told me of a lot of discord among the members of his medical practice group and talk of breaking up the practice. He had been with the group for several years, and the thought of losing his position there depressed him. As his depression worsened, he became concerned that his ability to practice medicine was impaired. I advised him to take a leave of absence from his practice, and I referred him to an excellent psychiatrist. With talk therapy and antidepressant medication, Al's depression was successfully treated. He resumed his successful medical practice.

As the years passed, he began to put on weight, confessed having a "sweet tooth," and said he felt chronically tired. As a physician, Al knew these symptoms were warning signs of type 2 diabetes. He consulted his physician, who confirmed the suspected diagnosis.

Recently, while talking with Al and his wife, Judy, they brought up the subject of Al's diabetes. They described how irritable he became when his blood sugar is out of control. I asked them if they knew, without relying on blood tests, whether Al's diabetes was also out of control. "Oh, yes," Judy promptly answered. "We know when his blood sugar is up because he gets so depressed, irritable, and tired, and his thinking gets cloudy. You know, he's always had twice as much energy as me. I couldn't keep up with him, and still can't when his diabetes is controlled. But when it's out of control, it's a different story. I can run circles around him. When we were on our most recent vacation, he ate too many sweets, and his blood sugar soared out of control. His thinking was so cloudy that he couldn't drive. I had to drive home."

As strong as these impressions were, they were just that—impressions, anecdotes. Not hard facts. Skeptics might rightly question the assumption of a specific cause and effect relationship between depression and diabetes by arguing that *anyone* with a chronic illness could be depressed. In other words, depression is an emotional response to having diabetes. Common sense suggests that this could be true in some cases. But my clinical impressions were strong. In an effort to learn more about the topic of diabetes and depression, I reviewed the literature. I found observational, experimental, and epidemiological data that shows a connection between impaired glucose metabolism and depression.

Let's look at this evidence under a magnifying glass.

Historical Literature on Depression and Impaired Glucose Metabolism

I knew that my idea—that impaired glucose metabolism often causes depression—was not original, but I did think the concept was relatively recent and under-appreciated. I expected to find little in the ancient, historical medical literature on this topic, but to be thorough, I decided to review the old literature extensively nevertheless. To my surprise, I found much more information than I had expected. Reviewing the historical literature was like taking a sip of water from a fire hydrant.

I was delighted—and I must confess, a bit chagrined—to learn that over 350 years ago, one of the first physicians to describe diabetes, Englishman Thomas Willis (1621–1675), had observed that in some people depression precedes diabetes. He wrote, "Sadness or long sorrow [. . .] often generate or foment this morbid disposition [diabetes]."

In the 1800s measuring blood sugar required large amounts of blood, which limited research. By the early 1900s, however, several techniques had been devised that allowed the precise measurement of sugar in small amounts of blood. This allowed investigators to measure glucose levels at several intervals and to compare blood sugar "curves" in various conditions. This advance in technology set off a veritable flush of enthusiasm in several countries.

In Germany, two impressive articles were published in 1919 and 1920. In 1919, Dr. Heidema reported that ten of seventeen depressed patients had an elevated blood sugar.[1] In 1920, Dr. Wuth found that blood sugar was elevated in eighteen of thirty depressed patients.[2]

In Holland, a Dutch physician, Kooy, reported in 1919 on his study of nineteen patients with melancholia (depression), eleven with mania, and twenty normal controls.[3] An elevation of blood sugar was most common in the depressed group.

In England in the early 1920s, two doctors, Drury and Farran-Ridge, studied the blood sugar curves of 100 mental states and found confusion and depression were most often associated with the greatest disturbance of sugar metabolism.[4]

Also in England, London physician Dr. S.A. Mann wrote a treatise on the topic that was published in 1925.[5] From his review of 104 scientific articles, he observed, "It is a generally accepted fact that the frequency of (impaired glucose metabolism) is greater in those mental states associated with melancholia (depression), and especially with stupor (lethargy)."

Dr. Mann designed an elegant study to test this prevailing view. He gave a sugar-containing drink to 152 patients (45 male, 107 female) who had been admitted to the Maudsley Hospital in London, England. Diagnostically, the group was heterogeneous, with a large number suffering from depressive "stupor."

Dr. Mann knew that blood sugar in normal people rises after ingestion of carbohydrates. Thus, the amount of sugar in the blood at any one point in time is of limited usefulness in determining whether sugar metabolism is impaired. A better measure is how fast glucose is being removed from the bloodstream (metabolized), and he determined this by measurements at frequent intervals, following the ingestion of glucose.

After the patients ingested a sugar-containing solution, Dr. Mann measured blood sugar levels at baseline and at fifteen-minute intervals for two and a half hours. Mann demonstrated that blood sugar peaked soon after ingestion of glucose in normal controls and in the patients. The difference was, however, that in normal people the blood sugar level fell to normal levels in two hours, while blood sugar remained high in those patients with depression. This was a clear and early indication that burning blood sugar is slower in depressed patients than in non-diabetic people without depression.

Back in those days, the basic defect was thought to be failure of the body to burn blood sugar. But, the cause of the impairment was not known. Dr. Mann reasoned that the defect lay in a "defective pancreatic reaction." In the early 1920s, Drs. Frederick Banting and J.J.R. MacLeod proved his theory. They isolated and purified insulin and injected it into patients with diabetes, with life-saving results. The amount of sugar in their blood fell, indicating that their bodies were now able to "burn" glucose.

Moreover, both Banting and MacLeod commented on the relationship between impaired glucose metabolism and depression.

Dr. Banting, in his Nobel Prize acceptance speech, noted that after administering insulin, "the pessimistic, melancholy diabetic becomes optimistic and cheerful."[6]

Dr. MacLeod, in his Nobel acceptance speech, commented on the "striking relationship between the concentration of glucose in the blood and the normal functioning of the nervous system. . . ."[7]

By 1931 so much research had been conducted on impaired glucose metabolism that two Wales researchers obviously felt a need to justify further research on this topic.[8] They wrote, "It may be thought this line of research has been exhausted by the numerous workers in the field . . . [because already] it has been reported that a certain percentage of melancholics [depressives] . . . show sustained hyperglycaemia [high blood sugar] after glucose ingestion."

In another review of the literature, published in 1939, two other researchers reviewed ninety-four articles on "manic-depressive psychosis."[9] They concluded, "There is striking evidence of disturbed carbohydrate metabolism . . . in the depressed cases."

Laboratory Evidence Linking Depression and Impaired Glucose Metabolism

One criticism of early studies stated that because glucose was taken by mouth the differences in blood sugar levels might be due to differences in absorption from the intestines. In 1958 Dr. I.G. Pryce administered glucose to nineteen depressed patients through their veins and demonstrated that in depressed patients the speed of movement of glucose from the bloodstream into cells is slower than normal.[10–11] This observation was confirmed by two other research studies.

By the 1960s, a test to measure insulin had become available (double antibody radioimmunoassay).[12] Using this new technique in the late 1960s, Dr. Peter Mueller and colleagues in the Department of Psychiatry at Yale University School of Medicine measured insulin levels and blood sugar levels in patients with endogenous depression, which is the type of depression that is chronic and in which an obvious, recent, external stress cannot be identified.[13] Endogenous depression is in contrast to reactive depression in which a recent stress can be identified. This study, published in 1969, also confirmed that glucose is burned slowly. *In addition, these researchers made a most interesting observation: The amount of insulin in the depressed patients' blood was elevated.*

Dr. Mueller's research group conducted another study and found that the depressed patients whose body movements were slowed were the ones who had impaired glucose tolerance. This was consistent with the findings during the early 1900s that "stuperous" or lethargic depressed patients were those most likely to have impaired glucose metabolism. Dr. J.H. Wright and colleagues—working at the Neuropsychiatric Institute at the University Michigan—also found that endogenous depression is associated with insulin resistance.[14] The response of patients to insulin was "blunted." In other words, the bodies of the patients were resistant to the action of their own insulin.

Dr. Mueller's article led to a fundamental shift in thinking. Earlier elevated glucose levels were thought to result from inadequate response of the pancreas, resulting in too little insulin. Now, however, the culprit had to be found elsewhere. The pancreas was producing more than enough insulin, but the body was not responding to it.

When I was reading Dr. Mueller's article, the following phrase seemed to leap off the page: "Amitriptyline [an antidepressant medication] itself may significantly increase insulin sensitivity." Here was evidence that increasing insulin sensitivity helps depression and increasing insulin sensitivity is precisely what chromium does. I had a piece of the puzzle, a plausible explanation for how chromium helps depression by increasing insulin sensitivity. I found another article that demonstrated that fluoxetine, or Prozac as it is commonly known, can improve insulin sensitivity.[15]

The most recent study linking depression and diabetes was conducted by Dr. Andrew Winokur and colleagues in the Department of Psychiatry at the University of Pennsylvania School of Medicine and reported in 1988 in the peer-reviewed medical journal, the *American Journal of Psychiatry.*[16]

Dr. Winokur enrolled twenty-eight patients (twelve men and sixteen women) who had major depression and control subjects who did not have depression, diabetes, or a family history of diabetes. All patients drank a solution containing glucose (sugar), and every thirty minutes for five hours, their blood was tested for both glucose and insulin. One hour after drinking the glucose solution, glucose and insulin levels rose in both depressed and non-depressed subjects, indicating that the pancreas in both groups was capable of secreting insulin. In the control group of non-depressed persons who did not have a family history of diabetes, insulin and glucose levels began to fall after an hour, an indication of sensitivity in the body of insulin receptors to insulin, or insulin sensitivity, for short. But in the group of depressed patients, both insulin and glucose levels remained elevated longer than in the control group. Although the depressed patients were not diabetic, graphs of their glucose and insulin responses resembled that found in type 2 diabetes. In other words, the non-depressed patients were sensitive to the action of insulin, but the depressed patients were not. This was further evidence that depression and the type of diabetes (type 2) caused by insulin resistance are linked.

I continued my review of the literature. I found extensive evidence in the literature that supported my long-held impression that impaired glucose metabolism causes depression in some people, and that depression can be an early sign of type 2 diabetes.

Studies Showing Depression Can Be an Early Sign of Diabetes

I read two convincing epidemiological (population) studies that suggest depression may indeed be an early sign of diabetes, often preceding the development of diabetes by several years.

The first study was conducted by Dr. William Eaton and his colleagues at the School of Public Health at Johns Hopkins University.[17] Dr. Eaton began his long-term study with 3,481 people diagnosed with serious (major) depression. After thirteen years, the number of study participants had dwindled down to 1,897. All the remaining participants were interviewed. Of that group, eighty-nine had developed type 2 diabetes. This was more than twice the incidence expected in the general population. In other words, the study suggested that the people who had been seriously depressed are at increased risk of developing type 2 diabetes.

In a similar study, Dr. Norito Kawakami and colleagues in Japan followed 2,380 depressed male employees of an electrical company for eight years and found that forty-one of them developed type 2 diabetes.[18] Statistical analysis of this study indicated that, in general, people with moderate to severe depression have 2.3 times higher risk of developing diabetes than did non-depressed people.

The studies of Eaton and Kawakami did not distinguish between atypical depression and non-atypical (melancholic) depression. My experience tells me that if they had included only people with atypical depression the incidence of developing diabetes would have been higher.

Now I was ready to give chromium to other depressed patients. My very tentative theory was that George, Elizabeth, and Sara's depression was rooted in insulin resistance, and that chromium, by increasing the sensitivity of their bodies to insulin and improving their ability to metabolize glucose, had caused their antidepressant medications to be more efficacious. With this theory in mind, I looked forward to giving chromium to other depressed patients who were dissatisfied with their antidepressant medications.

PART FOUR

A Beautiful
New Vista

CHAPTER 19

An Undergraduate in Experience

*Each one of us, however old, is still an undergraduate
in the school of experience.*

—JOHN CHALMERS DA COSTA (1863–1933)
revered teacher and surgeon at Jefferson Medical College

Although I had over thirty years of experience as a psychiatrist and psychoanalyst, I felt like a beginner as I was contemplating giving chromium to other patients who had unsatisfactory responses to antidepressant medications. I was, in fact, a beginner in this new endeavor.

Five different persons had come to me at five different times, each of whom had a mixed response at best to antidepressant medications, with some relief but limited by the seemingly inevitable and undesirable side effects. I told each of them about my experiences with chromium's ability to help George, Elizabeth, and Sara. When I asked these patients if they would like to try chromium, they all said yes. Their experiences and stories are described below.

Elaine

Elaine, a fifty-year-old physician/scientist, was referred to me by her psychiatrist, who had heard about my preliminary findings on the use of chromium to increase the effect of antidepressant medication in depressed patients who crave carbohydrates.

During our first meeting, Elaine related her struggle with depression, weight gain, type 2 diabetes, and PMS:

She reported: "My depression, weight gain, and uncontrollable appetite started during my last pregnancy, almost thirteen years ago. I felt exhausted and sleepy almost all the time. The delivery was uncomplicated, and the baby was entirely normal. But my symptoms got worse, particularly during the fall and winter months. I continued to gain weight.

"Look at me now. I've gained over 100 pounds. I weigh over 200 pounds now. Would you ever believe that I used to weigh 100 pounds, loved to exercise, and was full of energy?

"My depression also started soon after the delivery. I'm not talking about just being sad. I'm talking about being in the pits, an awful black hole.

"I consulted a psychiatrist, who prescribed Prozac, but within a few days I developed serotonin syndrome, which was awful. I felt electriclike shocks running up my arms, my nose was running, and I had hot flashes. I was agitated and my heart was racing. I was shaking all over, sweating, and unable to concentrate. My husband later told me I was confused and not making sense, my face was flushed—or "red as a beet," as he described it—and my muscles were rigid.

"Obviously I stopped Prozac and my psychiatrist prescribed 100 milligrams per day of Zoloft. Although Zoloft has helped my depression somewhat, it interferes with my sex life. And it does not curb my appetite or stop my weight gain.

"Despite Zoloft, I feel very, very tired, with an almost uncontrollable tendency to fall asleep—even when driving or while lecturing to students. About six years ago, my family physician made a diagnosis of type 2 diabetes. Actually, I think I had it much earlier than that, but it was never diagnosed. I've also had PMS for most of my adult life. My depression and carb craving are worse during the week or so before my period.

"Last month my psychiatrist suggested I take chromium picolinate in addition to Zoloft. He had heard about your findings in that regard. I started it and within three days I felt immensely better. My psychiatrist seemed surprised by how much better I felt. He suggested I come to see you to see if my improvement could be documented under single-blind conditions. I stopped chromium last week and have started to feel tired and sleepy again."

Elaine Receives Chromium

I suggested to Elaine a three-month, single-blind trial during which she would receive either chromium or a placebo, and she would not know which. She would continue taking Zoloft each day. Building on the lessons I had learned from Elizabeth and Sara, I decided to carry out the trial over three month-long periods coinciding with her menstrual cycle in an effort to evaluate the impact of chromium on her premenstrual syndrome. Elaine signed a consent form.

During the first month of the trial, in addition to 100 milligrams of Zoloft per day, Elaine took 300 micrograms per day of chromium picolinate, and within three weeks she experienced a dramatic lifting of depression, as well as the absence of PMS. Elaine's energy level improved and her sleepiness was less of a problem.

During the second month, Elaine received a placebo (vitamin B_{12}) that was almost identical in appearance to the chromium tablets she had taken the previous month. For two weeks, she felt good, but during the third week her depression, sleepiness, and carbohydrate craving surfaced again. During the fourth week, she had "terrible PMS."

During the third month of the trial, Elaine took 300 micrograms of chromium picolinate per day and again experienced a remission of her depression and PMS. Furthermore, her craving for food was markedly diminished.

She said, "I think I can begin dieting now. I'm not so hungry and depressed as I used to be. I'm feeling closer to my husband, too."

My experience with Elaine was a convincing example of chromium's ability to help atypical depression. Moreover, because she had type 2 diabetes, it suggested the possibility that the underlying cause of her atypical depression was insulin resistance.

Now that I look back, I wish I had asked for reports of Elaine's blood sugar levels during the three-month trial to see if her type 2 diabetes improved along with the improvement in her depression and PMS. But at the time I was seeing Elaine, I did not know that chromium helps improve type 2 diabetes. The studies documenting chromium's role in the treatment of type 2 diabetes and gestational diabetes (diabetes related to pregnancy) were published later.

Alice

Alice, a young scientist in her mid-thirties came to see me after her previous psychiatrist moved to another state and referred her to me.

Alice described her difficulties in the following way: "I started having problems—severe stomach pain—when I was in my mid-twenties. At first I thought I was having PMS, but soon I realized that these episodes occurred throughout the month. I went to my family doctor, who said I had a 'nervous stomach and spastic colitis.' He prescribed a sedative, which did not help.

"I next went to my gynecologist, who couldn't find out what was wrong. I continued to have pains in my stomach—abdominal pains, I mean—that became almost unbearable. So I went to another gynecologist, who said I had endometriosis. He prescribed birth control pills, but they didn't help. He said my only other option was to have a hysterectomy."

She burst into tears and told me, "So that's what I did—I had a hysterectomy. Of course, now I can never have children."

After drying her eyes, Alice continued, "The hysterectomy relieved my symptoms for awhile, but they returned. I couldn't believe it. All that for nothing.

"My gynecologist, the one who did the hysterectomy, then made the diagnosis of residual endometriosis in my bowels. I underwent still more surgery, exploratory surgery. Some endometrial tissue was removed. But I still had the same symptoms—frequent bouts of pain in my stomach, bloating, and diarrhea.

"I then went to several other doctors. None of them was able to help me. Because my symptoms didn't respond to their advice and medications, and they couldn't find a definite physical cause for my problems, the doctors thought I was just pretending to be ill. One exasperated doctor even wondered if I was 'faking and getting mileage' out of my illness.

"All the frequent pain, bloating, and diarrhea got me down. It hurt so much I couldn't sleep. Most mornings I'd get out of bed exhausted, having tossed and turned all night. I felt I'd fallen into a black hole of despair. I got really depressed. That's when I started seeing Dr. [here she told me the name of the psychiatrist]. I saw him for therapy off and on for bouts of depression for the last ten years or so. That helped some, but he said my problems were probably very deep and suggested I undergo psychoanalysis. That's why I'm here."

I saw Alice during a long and painful course of psychoanalysis. Her suffering was eviscerating. She often teetered on the brink of suicide, standing on the balcony of a tall building with one leg over the rail, preparing to jump to her death.

During psychoanalysis, Alice gradually realized—in large part through an understanding of her dreams—that her father had sexually abused her as a child. Even worse, her mother had ignored the situation and not protected her. Both Alice and I were convinced that the abuse had contributed, in some obscure way, to her very real physical problems. Although she found four years of psychoanalysis very helpful, even life saving, it did not stop her gastrointestinal distress, severe insomnia, and depression.

I therefore prescribed 100 milligrams a day of Zoloft, but this made her diarrhea and abdominal pains worse. Next I prescribed 100 milligrams of Pamelor a day. But this only moderately reduced her symptoms. We paid careful attention to her diet, but were unable to link her bouts of abdominal pain to any particular food.

Because Alice's abdominal pains were so severe and refused to respond to treatment, I arranged for her to have a consultation with a specialist in gastrointestinal disorders. The specialist recommended that she increase Pamelor to 150 milligrams a day. But this was of minimal help, at best.

I next prescribed 100 milligrams of Elavil a day. I chose this old tricyclic antidepressant because it dries out the intestines and often causes constipation, a side effect that annoys many patients, but which might benefit Alice. She experienced some improvement. Her sleep improved somewhat but her bouts of abdominal distress continued to be a problem, although they were somewhat less severe. I increased the dosage to 150 milligrams per day. This dosage further slowed down her gastrointestinal tract and marginally improved her sleep as well. Yet, clearly Alice needed more relief.

Against this backdrop, I felt it was appropriate to discuss with Alice the possibility of her taking chromium. I explained to her that the addition of chromium to Zoloft had greatly helped four people but, based on my very limited experience, I was unable to suggest it would help her, and furthermore, I did not know whether it would make the Elavil more effective. But, I told her it was an essential trace mineral and it was safe. Perhaps she had much to gain and little to lose.

To my offer, she said, "Anything is worth a try. I'll try anything at this point."

I also explained to Alice that because the use of chromium for depressive illness was only now being studied, I wanted to rule out a placebo response by administering several essential vitamins and minerals individually on a weekly basis in a single-blind fashion. As a scientist, she knew that the single-blind design meant I would know what she was taking but she would not. She readily agreed to my proposal. Alice continued taking 150 milligrams of Elavil during the length of the trial.

The first week, Alice received one 500-milligram vitamin B_{12} tablet per day. Her insomnia, depressed mood, low energy, and difficulty concentrating did not improve. The second week she took oyster shell calcium, and the third week she took vitamin C. For each of the three weeks, her bouts of diarrhea, bloating, gas, abdominal pain, insomnia, and depression continued. These bouts occurred as often as four to five times a week and left her exhausted the next day and barely able to function.

At the beginning of week four, Alice started taking one 400-microgram tablet of chromium picolinate each morning. They were almost identical in appearance to the vitamin B_{12} pills she had previously taken. Based on my experience with other patients, I had a hunch chromium might help Alice, but I was doubtful, as her suffering had been so chronic and so resistant to treatment.

I was surprised when, after only four days had passed, she reported the following: "My physical symptoms aren't as bad, and my depression is better. I'm not having nightmares, but my dreams are much more vivid. My sleep is restful. I wake up with plenty of energy for the day. To get a good night's sleep is wonderful. Colors appear richer. Food tastes good. My senses are keener. I'm able to enjoy things. I feel better than I have felt in twenty years. It's amazing."

My original plan was to discontinue chromium, and have her take oyster shell calcium again. But, because her description of her responses to chromium was so like that of George, Elizabeth, and Sara, I was convinced chromium was helping her and that stopping it and beginning oyster shell calcium would be putting experimentation ahead of treatment. I told Alice that, given her improvement, we should end the trial, and she should continue taking the current nutrient.

To my surprise, she said, "No. I want to go on as we planned. I'd like to know if this is a fluke."

During the fifth week, I discontinued chromium and gave Alice oyster shell calcium. Her symptoms of depression, insomnia, and exhaustion returned. When I gave her chromium during the sixth week, again these symptoms disappeared.

I could hardly believe it.

I told Alice that she had been taking chromium during the fourth and sixth weeks. The benefit was unmistakable, so we decided the trial should end and she should continue taking chromium. She agreed. Major changes in Alice's life came quickly. Her mood improved. The frequency of abdominal distress greatly lessened, her sleep improved, she felt rested during the day, and her depression was replaced by periods of joy. With these physical and emotional symptoms in the past, she was able to function at work to her full potential. She won an achievement award and accepted a major promotion that required her to move to another state.

I still hear from Alice occasionally. She tells me how much better she feels, how much psychoanalysis, chromium, and medication helped her, and how she is able to experience joy on many occasions. As of this writing, she has taken Elavil and 500 micrograms per day of chromium picolinate for five years and has remained symptom-free, with only an occasional and brief reappearance of depression, mild bloating, abdominal cramps, vomiting, and diarrhea.

Alice had suffered the agony of the damned. To see her released from her misery was a great relief for me, too.

I mailed Alice this chapter section for approval for publication. She verified its accuracy and gave me written permission to publish her story.

She added, however, "Chromium has helped me enormously, but it was not just chromium that was necessary. Please tell your readers, if you publish my story, that psychoanalysis, eating a good healthy diet, getting enough exercise, and taking medication also played major roles in lifting my depression. I just don't want the reader to go out, buy chromium, expect a miracle and forget that getting over depression requires a lot of hard work."

I wrote to Alice that I totally agreed with her and appreciated her suggestion. I wrote her that—although I think taking chromium is essential in the treatment of atypical depression—I, too, did not want anyone to rush out to buy chromium, thinking it was a "magic bullet," a cure-all, and to neglect other parts of a treatment plan.

Jim

I wondered if Jim, a man in his mid-forties, might benefit from chromium. He was referred to me by his brother-in-law, who was afraid Jim was going to commit suicide. He said Jim's marriage had failed and he had a pattern of working at "part-time, minimum-wage jobs, which he loses one after the other."

During our first meeting, Jim was disheveled and appeared depressed. I asked him to tell me about himself.

He said, "I'm a depressed person, a loser. That's just the way I am. No one likes me and I can't blame them. I'm tired all the time. Everything is a chore. The world would be a better place without me. My brother-in-law, who is a physician, said I looked awful, and asked me what was wrong. I told him how I felt and said that suicide was the only choice I had. He insisted I see you, to at least give this a chance. I told him I had seen several psychiatrists over the years, that nothing seemed to help, but he kept after me, and I agreed to see you at least once."

From this point on, I met with Jim for several years. As usual, the process began with efforts to understand his current symptoms and his early life. He described his early life as quite unstable. "Mama was volatile. She would fly into rages for no apparent reason, and frequently beat us children, especially my younger brother. Guess that's why he's a basket case, too. Dad was kind, but passive. He had his own problems and didn't protect us from her. Both of them had high expectations for me, but I failed to live up to them."

As Jim talked during our weekly meetings, he consistently dismissed his own abilities, stating he wasn't as smart as most people and had limited athletic ability. He felt he had failed both his parents. His mother had wanted him to be a banker or a doctor. For awhile he seemed to be on course for one of these careers. Jim's father wanted, and expected, him to play in the NFL. When I asked in more detail about his academic record and athletic ability, I learned that he was a straight-A student at a competitive college and was a record-setting athlete.

Why had none of his previous successes stamped his personality with a strong sense of self-worth? Psychiatrists are taught to remain detached and objective in order to avoid being flooded by a patient's suffering, but I was unable to avoid feeling sad when I heard Jim describe his painful feelings of worthlessness and aloneness. Once he said, "I had a day of vacation, so I went to the beach, alone. I rented a motel room and unpacked. I went out on the beach and sat on my lawn chair. I saw young couples walking hand in hand. And families. Children. Just reminded me how alone and miserable I am, and that I've been homesick all of my life."

I could almost feel his anguish, but I did not let my sympathy interfere with analysis. I forced myself to ask him the difficult question, "That sounds so painful. But perhaps you are not as helpless as you feel. Might you play a hand in bringing suffering down on yourself? Might you have internalized your mother's cruelty?" We spent many hours analyzing this question, and bit-by-bit over a long time, we gleaned the following.

Jim's inclination to punish himself, to put himself down, to minimize or ignore his talents and accomplishments, is known as moral masochism. We came to understand his masochism as a compromise formation between his opposing wishes to protect his mother and to hurt her, with several purposes. At the core was rage toward his mother, which he short-circuited by raging at himself instead. At the same time, he was actively disappointing her by failing to live up to her expectations. His mother preferred him to his father, which stimulated his love for her and competition with his father. He opted out of this conflict by degrading himself.

Another force behind Jim's self-defeating behavior was his feelings of competition with his younger brother, whom the mother beat mercilessly. When his mother was beating his brother, Jim would misbehave and become a "lightning rod" that could absorb the violence.

Treatment with Medication

Jim found our talks helpful, but it was obvious that he needed more, as he continued to suffer from chronic depression of mild to moderate intensity. Eventually I prescribed Wellbutrin (200 milligrams per day) and lithium (900 milligrams per day). Jim developed muscle twitching, and his depression only lifted slightly. We decided to stop both medications, and instead substitute an open-label trial (both he and I knew what he was taking) of 100 milligrams a day of Zoloft and 200 micrograms per day of chromium picolinate.

Jim Receives Chromium

Jim's symptoms of depression were almost completely relieved within one week. He reported feeling better than he had felt for years. We decided, however, to perform a trial in order to check if chromium was really making the difference. We decided that he would stop chromium and only take Zoloft. Jim's symptoms of depression returned within one month. Because of this, we decided to restart chromium at 200 micrograms twice each day, in addition to Zoloft. This dosage again relieved his symptoms of depression within a week. Jim's vivid dreaming was particularly noticeable during the second trial of chromium.

A Single-Blind Trial

I suggested to Jim that he stop taking chromium, to see if we could repeat his positive response by giving him several ingredients under the same single-blind conditions as I had done before with George, Elizabeth, Sara, Elaine, and Alice. He readily agreed to the plan.

He received oyster shell calcium, vitamin C, and vitamin B_{12}, each for one week, but he did not improve. But when chromium was added, his level of energy and mood improved. After the fourth week, chromium was discontinued, and again he received vitamin B_{12} pills that looked almost identical to chromium pills he had been taking. Within three weeks of discontinuing chromium and taking vitamin B_{12} pills, his symptoms returned.

When chromium was resumed, he correctly guessed, "I'm taking chromium now, aren't I? That vivid dreaming is back. I have more energy, I'm not so hungry, and I don't feel depressed. I feel normal, just like I did a few weeks ago when I was taking chromium."

I was intrigued by the vivid dreaming Jim reported. George, Elizabeth, and Sara had also reported vivid dreaming. This suggested to me that chromium was having an effect on the brain.

As of this writing, Jim has continued to take chromium for several years. There are no panaceas—no cure-alls—for wounds as deep as Jim's, and he continues to struggle with low self-esteem and loneliness. However, now he is working at a high-level, demanding job. He has enough energy to exercise regularly, and he has times when he feels confident about himself and cheerful.

Regarding our work together, he once said, "One difference between you and my parents is they expected me to hang the moon and were disappointed when I didn't. You think I had *already* hung the moon. Your positive view of me—and chromium—have helped me a lot. There are times now when I'm actually happy and self-confident. I feel normal. Thank you."

The last I heard from Jim his life was surprisingly better. He had married and he planned to take chromium picolinate indefinitely.

Chromium Fails

Two other patients tried chromium, but did not respond to it.

Jackson

Jackson, a middle-aged man whose profession required great dexterity, consulted me after separating from his wife. He developed a rapid-onset depression with insomnia and intense self-loathing. He had contemplated suicide. Because his depression had been triggered by a recent, obvious event (rejection by his wife), I assumed that a biochemical imbalance was not the main cause of his depression. Technically speaking, his diagnosis was "adjustment disorder with depression."

I recommended a once-a-week trial of psychotherapy, but he was uninterested. He reluctantly agreed to see me "three or four times." I told him I was not certain Prozac would benefit him, but prescribing it was a possibility. He rejected that recommendation, too, because he had heard from his professional colleagues that antidepressants impair digital dexterity, which he would not chance. I told him this was indeed true, but he could always stop an antidepressant if his hands began to tremble. He, nevertheless, preferred to postpone taking medication.

As an alternative I suggested he take chromium. He did so and took 200 micrograms twice each day for two weeks. But the chromium had no effect whatsoever. Eventually Jackson stopped taking chromium and finally agreed to take Prozac. This medication did not help, so he stopped it. He found a new woman friend and his depression lifted rapidly. I wanted to understand him better, but he saw no reason to continue the visits with me, so he decided to stop. I told him that my door is always open if his symptoms flared up again.

I wondered why Jackson had not responded to chromium. I considered one obvious difference between Jackson and the patients who had responded to chromium. Jackson was very thin. He had always been "wiry," as he described himself, and he had never been bothered by excessive appetite or weight gain.

Mary

Mary, a medical researcher in her early thirties, consulted me because of a panic attack. She described the incident: "I was about to board a plane and I got so nervous I didn't know what to do. I was shaking. Couldn't get my breath and I forgot who I was. I didn't know anyone I could call for help. Afterwards I felt so down and depressed. Life is not worth all of this."

I asked Mary to elaborate on the phrase, "I didn't know anyone I could call for help."

She explained, "I have been fiercely independent for as long as I can remember. At least as early as four or five. I remember growling at my parents back then, literally growling like an animal."

I said to her, "For a moment, I thought you said 'fear of dependence' rather than 'fiercely independent.' I guess that tells us what I'm thinking."

Mary—quick and bright—answered, "I think I know what you're getting at. I'm afraid of relying on people. Needing someone—or being in love—is dangerous. I don't know the difference between being in need and being in love. I carefully planned my first sexual experience with a stranger, knowing there would be no strings attached, no intimacy, so I couldn't get hurt. Every relationship I start ends up as a battle."

I said to Mary, "If we work together over time, I suspect that we will battle, too. I hope we can manage it."

Background

I asked her to tell me as much as she was able about her family and what in her background had caused her to be so afraid of intimacy.

Mary said, "Mother was so stiff, proper and proud, insisting I fit in with the country club set. Her focus was on what she wanted me to be, not on who I was. She was always picking on me. 'Don't do this! Why didn't you do that?' Always so negative! I think Dad was afraid of her and never protected us from her.

During my teens and twenties, I was a hell-cat, always bristling for a fight. But during my early thirties my anger gave way to anxiety and depression. There was one failed relationship after another. I got little pleasure out of life. Didn't seem worth living."

Course of Treatment

Mary started a course of psychotherapy with me. In addition, I prescribed an antidepressant medication, Tofranil, which she took before flying. Mary found her treatment beneficial in many ways. Her anxiety subsided and her relationships with others improved. But, in spite of the progress we made, her depression remained.

As a medical researcher, Mary was aware of the side effects usually associated with antidepressant medications and was loath to take any on a regular basis. At that point, I told Mary about my recent experience with chromium and suggested she take 400 micrograms per day. Her depression lifted immediately, within twenty-four hours, but within three days, her anger returned and "it made me impossible to be around." Therefore, she stopped chromium for three weeks. Her depression returned. I suggested that Mary resume chromium, but take only 200 micrograms per day.

Within one week, she said, "I am so angry I can't live with myself. And I feel hyper, almost manic."

Although she was not clearly manic, she did have a family history of manic-depressive illness and I was concerned that chromium might trigger a manic episode in her. Therefore, we decided to reduce the amount of chromium to 100 micrograms per day but again, within three days her anger returned as it did when she was taking the larger amounts.

I wondered what explained Mary's exquisite sensitivity to chromium. Her grandfather was "a manic-depressive who committed suicide," and perhaps Mary's anger outbursts were a manifestation of an underlying manic-depressive (bipolar) tendency. I discussed Mary's case with Dr. Golden, who commented, "I've always said, if a medication lifts depression, it can cause mania. This may be the most convincing evidence yet of chromium's antidepressant properties."

Although chromium lifted Mary's depression, she was unable to take it because it energized her too much and made her angry.

Mary had a successful outcome inasmuch as her symptoms of anxiety and depression diminished. She was eventually able to marry and have the children for whom she had longed but had been afraid to conceive.

When I sent this chapter to Mary for her approval she called me and said, "Yes, you have my permission to publish my case history. I was thinking about our relationship just the other day. You and I were warriors. I was fighting for distance and you were fighting for closeness through understanding. I'm glad you won."

I responded, "I prefer to think of it as *we* won."

A Puzzle

Why did Alice, Jim, and Elaine, as well as George, Elizabeth, and Sara respond to chromium, but Mary and Jackson had failed to respond?

The patients who responded to chromium had atypical depression, with a craving for sweets, were mildly to severely overweight, and lacked energy. Elaine had overt type 2 diabetes. All of them had a family history of diabetes and/or heart problems.

Mary and Jackson, by contrast, were thin, "wired." They never had to worry about excessive appetite or weight gain, and they did not have a family history of diabetes.

Soon after several more patients had responded to the addition of chromium to their antidepressant medications, Dr. Golden, Dr. Gaynes, and I wrote an article with the main emphasis on chromium's enhancement of antidepressant medications in the treatment of chronic depression. Lesser points were mentioned in the case histories and included chromium's ability to reduce excessive appetite, increase energy, increase dreaming, and alleviate PMS. At the time, we did not know how important these "minor" points would become. The article was published in the *Journal of Clinical Psychiatry* in 1999.[1] Abstracts of it appeared in *Psychiatry Drug Alerts* and *Review Series: Psychiatry.*[2–3] The article generated a lot of enthusiasm in the academic community. We received hundreds of emails from psychiatrists around the world who inquired about various aspects of the paper and confirmed our findings.

I thought my chromium journey had ended and I was pleased. Little did I realize that an even greater surprise was just around the corner.

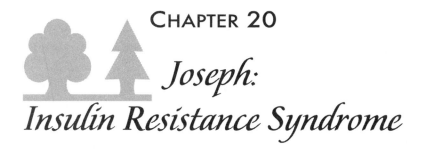

CHAPTER 20

Joseph:
Insulin Resistance Syndrome

The education of the doctor, which goes on after he has his degree is, after all, the most important part of his education.

—JOHN SHAW BILLINGS (1838–1913), *surgeon and co-founder of the National Library of Medicine*

My first contact with Joseph started in the early-1980s when I heard my office phone ring early one morning. I picked up the receiver and heard a woman almost yelling in urgent tones, "My husband is banging his head against the wall and is biting his arm. He's extremely depressed. He's having a nervous breakdown. I called our family doctor and he gave me your name. Will you please see him?"

I quickly scheduled an appointment with Joseph for early the next day. This was long before I had discovered the role of chromium in the treatment of depression and before I was aware of the connection between chromium and insulin resistance.

Our First Meeting

A few minutes before the appointed time, I heard my waiting room door open. I went out to greet Joseph. He was pacing about and wringing his hands. I noticed that he was thin. I introduced myself and invited him into my office. As we walked into the office, Joseph thanked me for seeing him on such short notice.

After we were seated, I began the interview with the following statement and question: "Your wife told me on the phone how upset you are. Can you tell me about it?"

Joseph answered, "I'm depressed, really depressed."

I said to him, "I want to help you. To do that, I must find out as many details as possible about your depression so I can determine what type it is. Depression is just like fever; there are many causes of it. First, I'd like to ask you, 'When did your depression start?'"

Joseph answered, "It started in my teens and got worse during my twenties. I'm thirty-four now. I'm depressed almost all the time. Once or twice a month I sink into such a pit of despair that I avoid all conversation, lock myself in dark rooms, and even bite myself and bang my head against the wall. If I keep having these outbursts of anger at work, I think both my career, which is really taking off well, and also my marriage will end soon."

I was surprised. Due to the severity of his symptoms and because he was thin, I had suspected he would describe melancholic depression in which the onset is rapid, the person loses weight, and the depression begins in mid-life.

Because early age of onset is characteristic of atypical depression, I wondered if Joseph might have other symptoms of atypical depression. Therefore, I said to him, "Some people who are depressed lose their appetite, while others have an increase in appetite. Some people are indifferent to what others say or do, while some depressed people are very sensitive to people around them."

At that point Joseph readily answered, "I'll try to answer your questions in terms of how much each of the symptoms bothers me. First, I'm way too anxious around people, and I'm too sensitive to what they say to me or how they act. I see and hear criticism in how people act and in what they say. It's really gotten me in trouble at work. I blow up and stomp away. I've been very successful at work, and so management has done everything possible to keep me. But if I don't get a grip and stop being so touchy, I'm going to lose my job. And my wife is at her wit's end, too."

In people with atypical depression, rejection sensitivity and being uncomfortable around people often begins during the teenage years or earlier, so I asked Joseph, "When did your problem of being uncomfortable around people begin?"

He fidgeted, as if the mere thought of people made him tense, "For as far back as I can remember. I think it was present even before I entered the first grade."

"Can you cite an example?" I asked, hoping to get a vivid example of his discomfort around people.

Joseph seemed to become even more anxious, winced, and said, "Yes. In the third grade, the teacher asked each of us to tell the class about our hobby. Mine was puppets and ventriloquism. I was afraid to stand before the class, so I practiced and practiced. When I started my demonstration before the class, one of the puppets fell off my hand. The children burst out in laughter and I've never felt so ashamed. Even today when I remember that incident, I have a twinge of pain. I dread being around people and having to interact with them.

"And you asked about my appetite. You wouldn't know it from looking at me 'cause I'm not overweight, but I'm hungry almost all the time, especially when I get anxious. That's a big problem for me and has been for many years. I have a sweet tooth and have craved sweets since I was a child. Back when I was in graduate school, my weight ballooned up to 200 pounds. At that time, to control my weight, I started on a low-calorie, high-protein, low-fat, low-carbohydrate diet. That controlled my weight, but I was always so tired and didn't have enough energy. To overcome being too tired, I gradually began to eat more sweets, especially cookies, candy, and several fruits each day. There's no telling how much I would weigh if I didn't exercise so much."

His comment that he felt exhausted alerted me to another sign of atypical depression, which is a feeling that the arms and legs are weighted down, so I asked Joseph if his arms and legs ever felt heavy.

He answered, "I'm tired almost all the time. My arms and legs actually feel heavy. I don't know how to describe it. I can move them, but it feels as if I'm not going to be able to."

I wanted to help Joseph describe the sensation in his arms and legs, so I told him about the story of a patient who was sitting in the office of a New York psychiatrist trying to explain the sensation of heaviness in his legs. The patient said, "You've seen those joggers around Central Park with lead weights wrapped around their ankles. Well that's how my arms and legs feel like." The psychiatrist used the term "leaden paralysis" to describe the sensation. I told Joseph about the patient's description.

Joseph emphatically agreed, "That's a perfect description of how my legs feel. I never knew quite how to describe it. It reminds me of one of the characters in Dante's *Inferno* who had to wear coats of lead. That's how I feel. And the more depressed I am, the heavier my arms and legs feel. So that's a characteristic symptom of my type of depression? What causes it?"

"Yes that is a symptom that many people with atypical depression have, but I regret to say that I don't know what causes it."

He learned forward, clasped his hands, and asked: "What is atypical depression?"

"Sorry, I should have explained," I said. "Atypical depression is a type of depression that is anything but atypical. It is actually a misnomer because it is the most common type of depression. Before atypical depression was described, for centuries it was believed that loss of appetite, weight loss, and severe insomnia were typical of depression. When depression associated with an increase in appetite and weight gain was first described around fifty years ago, this subtype was designated as atypical. It's an unfortunate term, but we're stuck with it, at least for now. But again, I can assure you, it is anything but atypical. It is estimated that half of depressed people suffer from atypical depression."

By now I felt fairly certain that Joseph had atypical depression, but wanted to get a fuller picture of his symptoms, so I asked, "I'd like to ask some more questions. Another symptom of atypical depression in some people is excessive sleepiness. Have you been bothered by that?" I asked.

Joseph shook his head and continued, "No. Just the opposite. Especially during my graduate school days, I would stay up almost all night. Many a time I left the lab to meet fellow students who were coming in for breakfast. Does that mean I don't have atypical depression?"

"No," I answered. "Atypical depression is a cluster of symptoms. Some people have one or two of them and others have more. Your depression started early in your life, you're sensitive to rejection, your arms and legs feel heavy, and your appetite is excessive. The only main symptom of atypical depression you don't have is excessive sleepiness. So it seems clear to me that the type of depression you have is the type known as atypical."

As the session was drawing to a close, I told Joseph that I wanted to make sure he was safe—that he would not attempt suicide.

He said, "I don't want to kill myself because I'm afraid of going to Hell, but I'm afraid I will because I get so desperate."

I was surprised by his answer. "You're afraid of going to Hell?" I asked.

He repeated what he had said and went into more detail: "Yes. I'm afraid of going to Hell. I think I detected a note of surprise in your voice that I, an educated person, believe in Hell. Well I do. I know there is a

Hell on Earth because I've lived in it most of my life, so it seems reasonable to me that there is a Hell after death."

"Are you able to promise me that you'll call if you get so upset you can't restrain your suicidal impulses?" Joseph promised that he would do this.

With that promise, our first session ended.

As Joseph was leaving my office, his description of his torment reminded me of the poignant words of Robert Burton, a scholar at Oxford University during the latter part of the sixteenth and first part of the seventeenth centuries and a lifelong sufferer from depression. He wrote, "If there is a Hell on Earth, it is to be found in a melancholy [i.e., depressed] man's heart."

Second Session

At the beginning of our second session, Joseph volunteered that he felt somewhat better already.

He said, "Just knowing that help is available has calmed me down some. And you seem to know what type of depression I have. Just putting words on it, being able to describe it, establishing some order relieves me."

"I'm glad you feel somewhat better, and I'm glad I'm able to describe your type of depression, but I don't know what is causing it. We need to find out more about your depression." I continued, saying, "Some people with atypical depression also have a problem with anxiety in social situations and panic attacks. Do you?"

Joseph answered, "I'm anxious around people a lot and I've had two or three panic attacks."

"Would you describe to me how you feel when you have a panic attack?" I asked.

Again he winced and reported, "About two years ago I had a panic attack, but I didn't know what it was or what is was called at the time. I was having dinner with my boss when, out of the blue, I was struck with an awful terror and felt electric-like currents surge down my arms, my heart started pounding, and I was short of breath. I thought I was having a heart attack and was dying. I was afraid I was going to faint, lose control of my bowels, and wet myself. They rushed me to emergency room where I had an EKG that was read as normal. The doctor told me that I had had a panic attack."

I asked Joseph if he had taken any substances that sometimes trigger panic attacks such as excessive caffeine, alcohol, monosodium glutamate (MSG), or amphetamines. He had not. In order to rule out a physical condition as the cause of Joseph's anxiety and depression, I asked, "Have you had a physical examination within the past year?"

He said, "Yes. I had a complete physical examination about six months ago, and the doctor told me I was normal, except for borderline high blood pressure. He said it was too early to treat it with medication, but we needed to keep a close check on it. If it went any higher, I would need to take some medicine for it. Otherwise, he didn't find anything wrong."

His high blood pressure puzzled me. In medicine, physicians look for one diagnosis that underlies all symptoms rather than looking for a separate diagnosis for each symptom. This scientific principle is known as "Occam's razor," or the principle of parsimony. But I did not know how, or if, Joseph's high blood pressure fit in with atypical depression. I tucked this fact away in the back of my mind.

I continued the interview by asking if he had ever sought treatment for depression, or if he had even taken an antidepressant medication.

He looked down and then met my gaze. "Yes. Once I went to see my family doctor because my throat felt tight. He must have thought I was depressed because he prescribed Elavil. It made my thinking fuzzy, and in my profession that is unacceptable. I definitely refuse to take an antidepressant."

Joseph's "bad" experience while taking Elavil, which is a tricyclic antidepressant, is another feature of atypical depression and it was noted in the 1950s.

Joseph's Background

I wondered to what degree his extreme rejection sensitivity was caused by inherited traits and how much was caused by his upbringing. I asked, "Will you tell me about the early years of your life. Where did you grow up? What were your parents like?"

Joseph answered, "Mom had two children who died soon after birth. I was her third. I was sickly as a child, and she hovered over me. She was a nervous wreck. Like me. Everything freaked her out. If I got a cold, she acted like it was the end of the world. Now that I look back on it, I think Mom was afraid I would die, too, and that's why she overprotected me. She kept me in the house and didn't let me play with other children. Mom is alive but her health is declining. We were from the wrong side of the tracks. I had no athletic ability and no friends. About the only thing I had going for me was that I was smart. I graduated at the top of my class and got a scholarship to college. That's how I ended up down here."

"Are any members of your family troubled by depression?" I asked.

Joseph answered, "Well, I don't know. In the early years of my life, Mom worried about everything. She had terrible headaches; many foods made her sick. She was miserable. Later on she became depressed."

"Are there any other medical conditions that run in your family?" I asked.

Joseph readily answered, "Mom gained a lot of weight late in her life. Her brother and sister had type 2 diabetes. My dad's mom had diabetes. She even eventually had to have her leg amputated. Two of Mom's brothers died from alcoholism; one was from an alcohol-related wreck and the other from liver failure."

I didn't verbalize this to Joseph at the time, but a family history of alcoholism is often found in people with atypical depression. I also wondered if type 2 diabetes is common in the families of people with atypical depression, but at that time I was not aware of any literature on this topic.

Continuing Treatment

By now it was clear to me that Joseph was describing the symptoms of atypical depression, including excessive appetite, unexplained exhaustion with feelings of heaviness of the arms and legs, early age of onset of depression, and extreme sensitivity to rejection by others. Moreover, he had a family history of depression, diabetes, and alcoholism.

Joseph had made it very clear that he did not want to take any medication for anxiety or depression. I told him I certainly respected his position and, in any case, it would be premature if I recommended an antidepressant because I did not know him well enough. After meeting with him a few more times, I recommended a course of psychoanalysis, to which he agreed.

We began to meet four times a week, and did so for six years. A thorough description of the analysis is far beyond the scope of this book, but I want to make the following points.

We traced his sensitivity to criticism to his earliest years when he was given frequent enemas. He would get angry with his parents and scream and scream. He was also afraid he couldn't make it to the bathroom in time. Any event during his adult life that reminded him, unconsciously, of being subjected to and humiliated by these procedures, caused an outburst of rage. We found confirmation in his relationship (transference) to me; that is, he experienced me as if I were humiliating him. To avoid offending me and to relieve his own anxiety, he invariably used the bathroom before our sessions.

Joseph found this and other insights helpful. We were able to identify triggers for his outbursts of anger. Joseph told me many times how helpful analysis was to him. He said that without it, he would have lost his job and family, or even worse, he would have killed himself in a fit of agitation. As a result of psychoanalysis, we agreed that he became a better husband to his wife, and a better father to his four children. He became immensely successful at work as well.

But, as helpful as analysis was, his underlying sensitivity to rejection and the resultant depression persisted. From this I concluded that a substantial part of his rejection sensitivity was biologic or genetic in origin and would not yield to further psychoanalysis.

After meeting with him four days a week for six years, I felt he had derived maximum benefit from analysis and suggested we interrupt our work. After many sessions in which we both discussed this possibility, we both agreed. I told him my door would always be open to him if he needed to return. He thanked me and left.

Growth of Problems

Three years after we ended the initial phase of our work together, Joseph called me and said he needed to see me.

When he arrived two days later, I asked him to tell me what had transpired during the three years since we last met. He said that his depression, insatiable hunger, profound tiredness, and sensitivity to rejection had gradually worsened and that once again, his job and marriage were threatened.

I suggested we resume meeting twice weekly. The psychological issues that we dealt with after resuming analysis were the same issues we had dealt with earlier: Joseph's vulnerability to criticism and his inclination to rage and despair after he felt devalued. Once again, analysis helped him cope more effectively at home and at work, but his underlying symptoms did not yield. I came to believe that Joseph was wedded to his symptoms that were very like his mother's symptoms. In other words, he was deriving attention from his symptoms and was therefore reluctant to let them go. After meeting for three more years, I again felt we had made as much progress as possible. Once again I told him that it was a privilege to able to work with him, but I thought he had derived maximum benefit from psychoanalysis and wondered if we should terminate. Both Joseph and his wife were frightened by my suggestion. There was no doubt in either of their minds that psychoanalysis was an emotional anchor for him, and without it, he probably would not be able to deal with life's difficulties. I agreed to continue to see him. He commented that "maintenance analysis" benefited him considerably at home and at work. But we were not learning anything new.

During this phase of our work, Joseph's blood pressure continued to rise. His family physician had prescribed two medications to control his high blood pressure. And he developed another problem: he had gained a lot of weight around his abdomen.

This time, I had a hunch that Joseph had insulin resistance, and it might be the cause of both his high blood pressure and his abdominal obesity. It was during this second phase of our work together when I learned that George and Elizabeth's depression had dramatically responded when they took chromium with an antidepressant medication. Immediately thereafter, I started to read as much as I was able to about chromium, and I learned that it was necessary for insulin to function normally. I also learned about some of the symptoms people develop when insulin does not function properly. To summarize, I learned that when the body is not sensitive to its own insulin, one or more of the following abnormalities result: abdominal obesity, high blood pressure, a decrease in HDL ("good") cholesterol, an increase in triglycerides, and an elevation of blood sugar. This condition is especially likely to develop in people who, like Joseph, have a family history of heart attack, high blood pressure, stroke, and type 2 diabetes.

After strongly suspecting that Joseph had insulin resistance, I asked myself the question, "Was it possible that insulin resistance was causing his depression and associated symptoms of excessive appetite and unexplained exhaustion?"

I explained insulin resistance to Joseph and told him about my budding theory that insulin resistance might be causing his depression. I told him that blood sugar must move into cells before it can be converted into energy. Insulin opens cell "gates" (insulin receptors) and allows glucose to enter where it is burned to produce energy. When the cell "gates" are "rusty" and do not open easily, the entry of blood sugar into cells is slowed down. This slowing down is called impaired glucose metabolism and can lead to type 2 diabetes, high blood pressure, stroke, heart attack, and in women, infertility due to polycystic ovarian disease. This results in a decrease in energy production and, I thought, it might explain why the large muscles in the arms and legs feel so exhausted; namely, they were deprived of energy.

I also explained that I thought his pancreas was detecting the problem of a decrease in energy production and was trying to force the cell gates open by producing large amounts of insulin. Apparently, his pancreas was strong enough to produce enough insulin to prevent blood sugar from backing up in his bloodstream. However, the large amount of insulin could be damaging his kidneys and causing them to retain fluid and salt, which in turn caused his high blood pressure. I also guessed that the high level of insulin, in some unknown way, was causing his depression.

Joseph agreed that my theory sounded reasonable and interesting. He asked what measures he could undertake that would alleviate insulin resistance. I told him that weight loss and eating fewer carbohydrates probably would help. I certainly advocated some fruit in ones' diet, although I believed he should decrease the eight or ten servings of fruit he ate each day. The sugar in the excessive amount of fruit he was eating was probably stimulating his pancreas to produce too much insulin. And the high level of insulin "dulls" insulin receptors and makes resistance to insulin worse, a vicious cycle.

As Joseph and I continued to work together, I discovered that several other patients, including Sara, had been helped by taking chromium with their antidepressant medication. At the time, I believed that chromium exerted its help by making antidepressants more effective and that chromium without an antidepressant would not be effective. I told Joseph that I did not think chromium would help him since he was not taking an antidepressant. But I added, on second thought, that all else had failed to relieve his depression and chromium was safe. Indeed it is an essential nutrient. Why not give it a try? I suggested this to Joseph.

With a shrug of his shoulders, he half-heartedly agreed, "What the heck, might as well try it."

Both of us were in for the surprise of a lifetime.

CHAPTER 21

The Sky Turns Clear and Blue

The joy of discovery is certainly the liveliest
that the mind of man can ever feel.

—CLAUDE BERNARD (1813–1878), *father of the scientific method in medicine*

When Joseph returned the next afternoon, he started the session by talking in hushed tones, almost as if he feared that revealing a precious secret would cause it to vanish.

He whispered in disbelief and confided, "I feel wonderful. When I got up this morning, I took 400 micrograms of chromium picolinate. On the way to work, the sky seemed so clear and blue. I felt like smiling. That's so unusual for me. By the time I arrived at work thirty minutes later, I was surprised because I felt light-hearted, another unusual thing for me. Imagine me, a shy "science nerd" who avoids people, being in the hall telling a joke to a co-worker. I haven't felt this good in over a decade, and during the rare times I have felt good, it lasted only a day or two."

I was stunned by his improvement because, in all the hundreds of sessions over several years, I had never seen him lighthearted and free of misery. I wondered about a placebo response, but somehow this did not appear to be a likely explanation, as nothing up to this time had helped his depression. Was it possible that chromium alone had lifted his depression, and had done so extremely quickly? He had only taken *one* 400 microgram chromium picolinate pill. I was not only stunned, but puzzled. What might explain his improvement?

I asked him if anything favorable had occurred in his life that had caused his improvement.

He answered, "No. In fact, I had a disagreement with a co-worker, and also my son made a low grade on his report card. Usually either of these events would have sent me into a tailspin. And, as you know, this is the anniversary of Dad's death and that used to make me sad, but not this year. My improvement is even more remarkable when considered in this context."

Still doubting that chromium was responsible for his improvement, I asked, "Can you think of any reason other than chromium that might explain why you feel better?"

Joseph, always the excellent scientist, answered, "The short amount of time from taking chromium to the lifting of my depression greatly reduces the number of possible intervening variables. I believe it is chromium that has helped me. I can think of no other explanation."

After our session ended, I pondered this startling change in Joseph. I didn't know what to make of it. I jotted down in my notes that "I'm relieved but puzzled that Joseph feels so much better. He suspects that chromium alone has lifted his depression. I'm afraid this won't last." I put my notes away and closed my office for the day. I would see Joseph again tomorrow. I expected his old depression would soon return.

An Important Piece of the Puzzle

The next day I went out to greet Joseph in the waiting room. His face had a pleasant expression and had no trace of his heretofore, usual furrowed brow.

Joseph began the session by speaking in the same hushed tones— almost a whisper—as he had spoken the day before. "My spirits are still good. And the strangest thing has happened. My dreams last night were supersaturated with color. They weren't unpleasant, just very rich in color. The surface of the images was shiny, wax-like, like plastic-coated with polyurethane. More color than you'd ever see in nature. Do you remember when Technicolor movies came out? How the colors seemed *too* colorful? My dreams are like that. I've never had a dream in my life that is so vivid and supersaturated with color. Usually my dreams are drab."

The vividness of his dreams sent me reeling, as it strongly suggested that chromium was acting directly on his brain. Somehow, people seem to intuitively equate depression with drab colors, commenting for example, "I feel so blue" and "It's so gray today."

Joseph had a similar thought, as he added, "This can mean only one thing: chromium is having a specific effect on that part of my brain having to do with color perception and depression."

I marveled at his extraordinary observation and asked him if the amount of time he had spent dreaming had increased. He thought it had, but he wasn't certain. The striking characteristic was the colorfulness of his dreams. I also wondered if that part of the brain having to do with color perception also involves appetite and energy regulation.

Joseph's report of colorful dreaming was easily the most dramatic moment I had had in the tens of thousands of hours I had spent listening to patients over a span of thirty years.

The reason I found the change in his dreams so impressive is because antidepressant medications often cause an increase in dreaming, and in some cases, nightmares.[1] In other words, vivid dreaming suggested that chromium, a dietary supplement, was acting on Joseph's brain as do antidepressant medications. George, Elizabeth, and Sara also had reported vivid dreaming after chromium was added, but I assumed the increase in their dreaming was due to chromium's boosting the antidepressant medications they were taking, not due to the action of chromium itself.[2] Was it possible that chromium by itself was increasing the amount of serotonin, or some other chemical, in the brain?

More evidence suggested chromium might be increasing brain serotonin. Drugs that stimulate serotonin activity in the brain cause a reduction in appetite.[3–5] George, Elizabeth, and Sara also reported a reduction in their appetites after beginning chromium. In fact, George had observed, "Whatever it is I'm taking [chromium] has reduced my appetite. [Chromium] is definitely improving the way my body is handling food because I'm not hungry all the time." But I also attributed the appetite suppression to the enhanced antidepressant effect, not to chromium acting independently. Time would tell.

As soon as I could, I contacted Dr. Golden by email and wrote, "The most remarkable occurrence. A patient of mine has responded to chromium alone with lifting of depression and vivid dreaming. I take this as evidence that chromium is exerting an effect on his brain. I wonder if chromium is increasing brain serotonin. More later." Dr. Golden replied, "Amazing."

Alternating Belief and Disbelief

Over the next two months, Joseph continued taking chromium. He said that chromium allowed him to feel better than he ever had in his entire adult life. I was astonished at the change in his feelings and behavior. He became increasingly positive that chromium had wrought this wonderful change.

He almost insisted that it was true, by saying to me, "Chromium is an effective antidepressant. And it's far better than the synthetic, pharmaceutical antidepressants because I don't have any side effects at all from it."

But I was less certain. One day I would find myself believing it was chromium that had lifted his depression, but the next day I would doubt it. I wanted more proof. Therefore, I suggested to Joseph that he stop taking chromium to see if his symptoms returned. If they did return, we would next set up a single-blind trial; that is, I would give Joseph various dietary supplements that he could not identify, but I would know which one he was taking.

I emphasized to Joseph the experimental nature of this proposed undertaking, and said that stopping a dietary supplement was not withholding a proven treatment. Moreover, if his symptoms returned, he could resume chromium. At first he was reluctant to stop chromium, as he was positive it had caused the lifting of his depression. But, I was less certain. Our disagreement eventually proved to be the case of the patient teaching the physician. Or, as the French novelist Marcel Proust observed: "Most of what physicians know is taught them by the sick."

Reluctantly, Joseph agreed to the plan I had suggested. He stopped taking chromium. His depression, tiredness, anxiety, and excessive hunger returned within one week. This immediate return of his symptoms astonished me and reminded me that George also had a rapid return of symptoms soon after stopping chromium picolinate.

Because of the return of his symptoms, we began the single-blind trial.

Single-Blind Trial

The first week, I gave Joseph vitamin B_{12} pills that looked almost identical to the chromium picolinate pills he had been taking. His symptoms persisted. He reported that he was "hungry, tired, had no interest in sex, and was worrying about everything."

During the second week, he received oyster shell calcium. In his weekend summary journal that he kept, he noted he was feeling "sad, anxious, fatigued, hopeless, and hungry, with a substantial sleep disturbance."

During the third week, Joseph received chromium picolinate. Within two to three days, he reported a dramatic improvement and disappearance of all symptoms. "I think I'm taking chromium again," he correctly guessed, "because those vividly colored dreams have returned and my depression is gone."

Again I was stunned, but the lifting of Joseph's depression under single-blind conditions removed all of my doubt. Chromium alone, taken without any antidepressant, had caused the relief of his depression. His response to chromium under single-blind conditions was almost identical to his earlier responses to chromium, namely lifting of depression and induction of vivid dreaming. I stopped the single-blind trial that day because stopping chromium and giving Joseph another ingredient would have been unethical at this point. The evidence that chromium alone had lifted his depression was overwhelming.

The Joy of Discovery

Right away I sent an email to Dr. Golden: "My patient's depression lifted under single-blind conditions when he took chromium alone. Now I'm positive that chromium alone is an effective antidepressant, at least for this one man. It is so gratifying to be able to help someone like this." Dr. Golden responded, "The only thing better than helping one person is helping millions of people."

While driving home that night, I heard myself laughing out loud in the car all by myself. Usually I would have been preoccupied with the issues raised by one of my patients. But on that night, I was filled with a curious mixture of elation and puzzlement. Had I found a natural substance, taken without an antidepressant, that might relieve depression in some people? Yes I had, but it seemed almost impossible. I reigned in my enthusiasm by reminding myself that only one patient, Joseph, had responded to chromium taken without an antidepressant. Or had George also responded to chromium alone? It seemed he might have, but I wasn't sure.

Hiding in Plain Sight

I pulled out my extensive notes on George and began to review them. And right there, hiding in plain sight in my notes, was George's observations that he felt better after he stopped taking his antidepressant medication and when he took chromium alone. Moreover, he stopped chromium on several occasions, and each time his depression had returned. Upon resuming chromium alone, his depression had lifted. As I continued to read George's notes, I found an assertion about the superiority of chromium over standard antidepressants that reminded me of an almost identical assertion Joseph had made.

George had written, "Before Zoloft I was tired and wanted to die. Zoloft helped my mood, but it made me feel slow in mind and body, and I still felt my life was behind me. After I stopped Zoloft and continued chromium alone, I see the life that is ahead of me. It's the first time I can remember being hopeful about the future. For me, chromium is a better antidepressant than Zoloft."

I had highlighted these observations in yellow, so obviously I had read them, and more than once. But somehow, for reasons that are unclear to me, I had ignored—or more accurately suppressed because of disbelief—George's observation that chromium alone had helped him. Perhaps I was so certain at the time of writing my notes on George that chromium increased the efficacy of antidepressant medications that I was blinded temporarily to the further discovery that chromium alone was exerting this antidepressant effect. As Dr. Claude Bernard wrote, "It is that which we do know which is the great hindrance to our learning that which we do not know."

Further Proof of Chromium Alone Relieving Depression in Joseph

As a "fast-forward" communication, Joseph remained free of depression for the next seven years after he first took chromium—except for two occasions. Both of these relapses were caused by stopping chromium. And both of them lifted as soon as chromium was resumed.

The first incident occurred when Joseph's chromium picolinate ran out and he bought another bottle. Within one week after beginning the new brand of chromium picolinate, his depression and tiredness and carbohydrate craving returned. In addition, the new brand of chromium made his entire body itch.

At my request, Joseph brought in the bottle of the ineffective chromium preparation. The label read simply: "Dietary chromium 200. Glucose tolerance factor. No yeast. No sugar. No starch. Kosher vegetarian." The manufacturer was not identified on the label.

Over the next several weeks, Joseph tried several brands of chromium picolinate. One had a bad odor, others had no effect, and one preparation upset his stomach. He and I began to suspect that there was great variation in effectiveness depending on the form and quality of chromium used.

Both of us set out to identify the original preparation to which he had so dramatically responded. Fortunately, Joseph had kept the empty bottle. He brought it in during his next session. The label identified the manufacturer as Nutrition 21. Joseph purchased another bottle of chromium picolinate made by the same company. After taking this original brand again, his symptoms lifted within three days, and he never took another brand of chromium again.

The second incident occurred when Joseph was advised by his family physician to stop all medication—including chromium—for one week before undergoing a medical procedure (colonoscopy). Joseph did so, had the procedure, and did not experience a return of his depressive and other troublesome symptoms for a week. I suggested that he not resume chromium, as he had not relapsed in one week and I suspected his body stores of chromium were now adequate. Joseph reluctantly agreed to this plan.

Gradually, over the next two months, he became mildly depressed. Then his depression accelerated rapidly and became as severe as it had ever been before starting chromium, with a return to head banging and locking himself in his closet. I was alarmed—and I felt guilty that I had suggested he not resume chromium immediately after his colonoscopy. I urged Joseph to resume chromium right away, which he did. As before, over the next three days after resuming chromium, his mood rapidly improved. He said he felt cheerful again. After one week, he said he was lighthearted, could joke with people, and felt content.

As of this writing, Joseph continues to take chromium. He says he never wants to be without it.

The Cause of Joseph and George's Depression

Joseph and George had some of the signs of insulin resistance, and both had responded to chromium alone. It seemed plausible to me that insulin resistance had caused their depression, and chromium, an insulin-sensitizing agent, had lifted their depression. Would other depressed patients with signs of insulin resistance—including I thought, carbohydrate craving—respond to chromium picolinate alone?

CHAPTER 22

Help from Experts

When thou arte call'd at anye time,
A patient to see,
And dost perceave the cure too grate,
And ponderous for thee . . .
Get one or two of experte men,
To helpe thee in that neede . . .

—JOHN HALLE (1529–1566), *English physician and writer*
who recognized the importance of second-opinion consultation

S oon after I learned that both George and Joseph had responded to chromium alone, I began to recommend chromium picolinate alone, that is, without antidepressant medications, to some of my other depressed patients who craved carbohydrates and who were troubled by unexplained tiredness.

I also told several of my colleagues about the role of chromium in the treatment of atypical depression. They, too, began to give chromium picolinate to their patients who had the signs of atypical depression. Some simply recommended chromium after telling their patients about the experiences of my patients.

Yet, some physicians and psychotherapists wanted to participate in double-blind studies in which neither the psychotherapist nor the patient knew if they were taking chromium or a placebo. To facilitate their efforts, I gave these healthcare professionals envelopes that contained either chromium picolinate or vitamin B_{12} tablets, which were almost identical in appearance to the chromium tablets. The envelopes were numbered, but neither the healthcare professionals nor the patients knew which envelopes contained chromium and which contained a placebo. Only after the patients had taken both placebo and chromium for one week each did I reveal whether the enveloped contained chromium picolinate or a placebo.

In several cases, the results were just as dramatic as those with Joseph. Patients who had suffered from atypical depression—some of them for years—showed relief from taking chromium picolinate alone within a few days.

Over the next several months, the number of depressed patients who had benefited from chromium swelled to perhaps 200. I became increasingly confident of my ability to identify people whose depression would—and would not—respond to chromium. Those most likely to respond had excessive appetites, unexplained exhaustion, and one or more of their blood relatives had type 2 diabetes or heart disease.

Several patients who responded to chromium had SAD or "winter blues," as it is often called. While the symptoms of SAD and atypical depression are similiar, they may be two different disorders. But I suspected that chromium is effective in the treatment of winter blues as well.

But how could I disseminate this discovery that chromium alone helps atypical depression?

Meeting with Drs. Golden and Davidson

Knowing that two or more minds are better than one, I contacted Dr. Golden and Dr. Davidson and asked them to meet with me. I had been in contact with both of them over the several months since I first made the discovery with George. Now that I had additional evidence that chromium alone was effective in depression, I felt it was time for all three of us to get together face to face. I explained that the purpose of our meeting was to present more data from my research, to interview three patients (including Joseph) who had responded to chromium, and to obtain their advice on charting a course of further investigation.

First I showed Drs. Golden and Davidson my extensive notes and data on several patients, especially those who had responded to chromium under double-blind conditions. They found the evidence compelling.

Next, I introduced them to Joseph, who had come to my office at an appointed time. I gave a brief outline of his background and our work together. I mentioned what a fine person he is and how he had pulled himself out of poverty and was now a leading scientist. I showed the doctors a copy of his voluminous and most impressive doctoral dissertation and

some of the publications that had helped to establish his excellent reputa-
tion. I also clarified that Joseph had come to this meeting not only will-
ingly, but eagerly, and reiterated what he had told me—that he had
encouraged me to make my discoveries widely known, as he hoped other
people would benefit as much from chromium picolinate as he had.

Next, we concentrated on Joseph's description of his response to
chromium. He told us about his battle with depression during all of his adult
life. He said that psychoanalysis had prevented him from committing suicide
and had helped him in many ways. But it had not helped his underlying
depression, lethargy, and craving for carbohydrates. He said that when he
took chromium, his depression lifted immediately and his dreams became
vivid. When he stopped chromium, his depression returned. When he took
chromium again, under single-blind conditions, his depression lifted.

Joseph concluded the interview with the following words: "I feel just
fine 97 percent of the time since I started taking chromium. Before chromium, I felt miserable 97 percent of the time. Chromium has helped me so
much that I want others to know about it. It is inexpensive and most
importantly, it does not have any side effects. In my opinion, because of
the absence of side effects, chromium is superior to synthetic antidepressant medications."

We thanked Joseph for his time and for his willingness to tell his story.
After he left, Dr. Golden emphatically stated that Joseph's improvement
was "extremely impressive and dramatic." Dr. Davidson agreed.

Even now, at the time of this writing, I have to pinch myself sometimes
to make certain I'm awake and not dreaming.

What to Do Next?

All three of us wondered what to do next. Dr. Golden said he would like to
co-author a paper with me on the use of chromium alone in the treatment
of depression, which we eventually did. We described the relief obtained
by eight depressed patients with carbohydrate craving when chromium
picolinate alone, that is, without an antidepressant medication, was administered. And we stated that our theory was that chromium helps depression
by increasing the sensitivity of the body to insulin and improving glucose
metabolism, which result in an increase in brain chemicals (catecholamines
and serotonin) involved in depression. The article was later published in
the peer-reviewed *International Journal of Neuropsychopharmacology*.[1]

At our meeting, Dr. Davidson said he wanted to conduct a double-blinded, placebo-controlled study to see if my observations that chromium alone relieves depression would hold up under the strictest standards of scientific research.

"But where can we obtain funding?" Dr. Davidson asked me. I told him that some months earlier, when I was discussing with Dr. James O. McNamara how chromium might work, Dr. McNamara, chief of the Department of Neurobiology at Duke University Medical Center, gave me some practical advice. He advised me to get patents covering my discoveries. Without patent protection, I would be unable to secure from a company the funding necessary to further my research. On the other hand, if I were able to obtain patents, a company might be willing to fund the research studies necessary to prove my discoveries under the most strict scientific standards. I had followed Dr. McNamara's advice and had obtained patents. Also, I had already contacted several companies to see who might be willing to support research. I was impressed with Nutrition 21 and asked them if they were willing to fund the Duke study.

As a result of conversations with several people at the company that had taken place months before the meeting with Drs. Golden and Davidson and with Joseph, they agreed that the data were indeed convincing and justified their funding a clinical trial. They asked me to submit a proposal for a grant to support such a study. The next question was, "Who would conduct such a trial?" I told them that I had in mind a world-class scientist and psychiatric researcher, Dr. Jonathan R.T. Davidson, professor of psychiatry at Duke University Medical Center. I told them about Dr. Davidson's credentials. He had conducted dozens of clinical trials and had published more than 300 scientific articles and two books. They were excited by the prospect.

I contacted Dr. Davidson and told him the good news. We began to design the study.

Overall Study Design

Dr. Davidson asked Drs. Kurian Abraham and Katharine Connor to be co-investigators in the study. They readily agreed. Along with Dr. Davidson, they would evaluate patients. Ms. Nabila Danish would be the study coordinator, who announces the study, answers telephone calls from prospective patients, screens callers to make sure they qualified for the study, welcomes potential subjects at the hospital, explains the study to them, and obtains informed consent.

We planned to enroll fifteen depressed persons who also had symptoms of excessive appetite or weight gain, tiredness, and/or sensitivity to rejection. Ten persons would receive 400 micrograms of chromium picolinate per day for two weeks, and, if they tolerated 400 micrograms per day without adverse effects, the dosage would be increased to 600 micrograms during the remainder of the study. The remaining five would receive a placebo or "dummy pill." Each person on the study would be followed for two months.

The study would be double-blinded and placebo-controlled. In other words, neither the investigators nor the study participants would know who was taking chromium or placebo until after the study was completed. The pharmacy at the Duke University Medical Center would keep the code identifying who was taking what, and that code would not be opened or "broken" until after the study was completed. By this means, any level of unintended bias was reduced.

To measure and keep track of the severity of depression, either Drs. Davidson, Connor, or Abraham would interview the persons every two weeks and ask the participants to fill out self-rating scales for severity of depression every two weeks.

Although I participated in the design of the study, I deliberately would never meet any of the persons enrolled in the study. I would not conduct any of the evaluations of them, nor participate in the evaluation of any results. The reason for my absence in these capacities was to eliminate any chance of my influencing the results. I knew I would not do this consciously—and hopefully not unconsciously—but in science, mere declarations of intent and objectivity do not count. Rather, what counts are the results of properly designed experiments.

Dr. Davidson submitted the proposal to Nutrition 21. After a short time, the company happily agreed to fund the study.

Obtaining Approval of the Institutional Review Board

The next step before beginning the study was to obtain approval of the Institutional Review Board (IRB) of Duke University Medical Center where the study was to be conducted.

IRBs are located in most scientific and medical institutions such as universities and research centers. The primary purpose of these boards is to protect the rights of research subjects. The main tenets of IRBs are as follows:

- Making certain that patients are not coerced into participating in research;

- Approving research only when risk is low and potential rewards are high;

- Fully informing subjects about the study;

- Obtaining written consent to participate in research; and

- Ensuring that effective, proven treatments are not concealed or withheld from the patients.

After a short time, the Duke IRB approved our proposal. A bridge had been built, paving the way for research on testing the effects of chromium alone on atypical depression. Now Dr. Davidson and I could cross to the other side. Although both of us were "up in years," we eagerly anticipated the beginning of the study with as much enthusiasm as two schoolboys.

CHAPTER 23

Proof: Evaluating Chromium Alone in the Treatment of Atypical Depression

The experiment is the most powerful and most reliable lever enabling us to extract secrets from nature. . . . [It] must constitute the final judgment as to whether a hypothesis should be retained or be discarded.

—WILHELM CONRAD RÖNTGEN (1845–1923)
German physicist and discoverer of the x-ray

To recruit volunteers for the study, the following advertisement was placed in a local newspaper in the fall of 2001:

ARE YOU DEPRESSED?

☐ Do you feel down?
☐ Do you have increased appetite and/or have you gained significant weight?
☐ Do you sleep too much?
☐ Do you feel exhausted a lot of the time?
☐ Are you easily hurt by rejection or criticism?

If you are age limit 18–65 years old, physically healthy and meet study criteria, you may be eligible for an investigational research study at Duke University Medical Center. We are evaluating a dietary supplement for the treatment of depression. Study-related care and psychiatric assessments will be provided free of charge to you.

For more information call
Nabila Danish, study coordinator at (919) 684-9701.

After running the advertisement only once, twenty-nine people answered the ad almost immediately. It was never necessary to run the ad again.

Setting Up the Study

This quick response—compared with the usual slow recruitment of volunteers for other clinical trials testing new synthetic, pharmaceutical antidepressant drugs—suggested to us that many persons might be dissatisfied with standard antidepressant medications and might be open to a natural treatment for depression. The rapid enrollment also underscored what we already knew, namely, that atypical depression is a prevalent type of depression.

The study coordinator, Ms. Danish, conducted a preliminary screening of twenty-nine people over the telephone to determine if they qualified for the study. She excluded ten people because they were taking an antidepressant medication. Two had scheduling difficulties, and one had an abnormal laboratory test. Of the sixteen persons who entered the study, one dropped out right away because of moving to another part of the country.

Criteria for Inclusion in the Study

Each of the sixteen participants came to the hospital for a personal interview, an explanation of the study, and for tests (EKG and lab tests) to make certain they were physically healthy. After being fully informed about the purpose and outline of the study, consent was obtained.

Standardized Scales and Guides

The study used standardized self-rating scales, interview guides, and evaluation guides. All of these were basic and well-known tests, which have been widely used for many years in various research studies and clinical trials. These tests assign numerical values to answers so that responses can be later analyzed according to accepted biostatistical methods.

Physician Interview and Evaluation Guides

Either Drs. Davidson, Abraham, or Connor interviewed each patient at the beginning of the study. They used two standardized interview guides: the "broad" Mini-International Neuropsychiatric Interview (MINI) to identify several disorders, including depression, and the Columbia Atypical Depression Diagnostic Scale (ADDS) to evaluate the severity of atypical depression.

In addition, one of the physicians evaluated each study participant at two-week intervals by using two standardized evaluation guides: the Hamilton Depression Scale (HAM-D) which, as its name suggests, measures the level of severity of depression, and the Symptom Occurrence Scale (SOS) to evaluate any side effects.

At the end of the study, one of the physicians repeated the ADDS evaluation to compare any change in the level of depression from the start of the study to the end of the two-month study period.

Self-Rating Scales

Besides the interview and evaluation by the physicians, study participants rated their symptoms every two weeks using two self-rating scales: 1) the Clinical Global Improvement (CGI) scale, which assesses overall or general improvement in depression, and 2) the more detailed Symptom Checklist 90 (SCL-90), which covers many emotional symptoms, not just depression. (This is the same scale I had given to George and Elizabeth.) Ms. Danish was available to answer questions anyone might have about how to fill out the scales.

Guidelines for Measurement of Amount of Relief from Depression

The cut-off point for numerical values that defined improvement from depression were selected before the study began. They were as follows:

- A decrease in the severity of depression as measured by a drop of at least 66 percent in numerical value on the HAM-D evaluation scale;

- Confirmation of improvement by a self-rating of "*very much improved*" on the CGI scale.

The Study Begins

Although I was positive that chromium picolinate was effective in atypical depression, I knew that if this study at Duke did not confirm my findings—for whatever reason—my discovery would never see the light of day and find its way to suffering people. And securing funding for another study would be almost impossible.

Midway through the study, I called Dr. Davidson and asked him how the study was going. He reported, "All three of us [meaning himself, Dr. Abraham and Dr. Connor] have observed a dramatic and rapid lifting of depression in some patients, but of course none of us knows whether they are receiving the placebo or chromium. We'll just have to wait and see after the trial is over and the blind is broken."

Stunning Results

Finally, the day came. On Friday, February 22, 2002, Dr. Davidson called to tell me that the study had been completed. The double blind had been broken, meaning that the code had been opened and now he knew which patients had been taking chromium and who had received a placebo.

The results were stunningly positive. In a voice filled with enthusiasm, Dr. Davidson exclaimed, "The results of the study strongly support your hypothesis that chromium helps atypical depression. A researcher waits an entire lifetime for a moment such as this!"

Early the next morning, Dr. Davidson came to my office, and we discussed the results in some detail.

Seven of the ten persons receiving chromium picolinate had met pre-treatment criteria for improvement from their depression, while none of those receiving the placebo had a positive response. The three patients who did not respond to chromium had no reaction to it whatsoever—either positive or negative. People do have different responses to different substances, whether they be medications, food, environmental factors, and the like. We did not know why some responded to chromium and others did not. But, for those who did respond, Dr. Davidson stated, while physically imitating putting a key into a lock and turning it, "It's as if chromium is a key that fits magically and perfectly into a lock, and relieves depression."

Of the seven who responded to chromium, the average HAM-D evaluation score at the beginning of the study was 29. This score indicates depression so serious that it is difficult for a person to function in his or her daily life. At the end of two months, the average score of those who responded to chromium was 5, which means practically no symptoms of depression. For all practical purposes, this score indicates that all traces of depression had disappeared.

The symptoms of the responders that were most consistently relieved by taking chromium were depressed mood, excessive appetite, excessive interpersonal sensitivity, and fatigue. In other words, the seven persons who took and responded to chromium reported a rapid and profound lifting of depression, a reduction in appetite, a decrease in sensitivity to rejection, and an increase in energy—all improvements in symptoms that characterize atypical depression.

Another remarkable observation was the speed with which the seven responders responded to chromium. By the time of the rating at the end of the first two-week interval, several persons had already experienced a dramatic lifting of depression. In contrast, standard synthetic antidepressant medications often require four to six weeks to relieve depression. This suggests that chromium acts faster and is therefore far superior in more quickly treating atypical depression than are pharmaceutical antidepressant drugs.

But perhaps the most hopeful result, which appeared in the seven persons who responded to chromium, was the absence of any physical or mental side effects. None. Therefore, this suggests yet another reason why chromium is superior to synthetic antidepressants.

Follow-up

After learning the results of the study, I felt a great sense of relief and comfort. The results of the study at Duke were almost identical to what I had observed in my patients. To have my observations confirmed by independent researchers using a sophisticated and reliable study design was a day—and a most marvelous feeling—that I will never forget.

Drs. Davidson, Abraham, Connor, and I later wrote an article describing the study, which showed chromium's positive effect on atypical depression. It was published in the peer-reviewed medical journal *Biological Psychiatry*.[1]

Now there was time for me to reflect, tie loose ends, and offer some practical advice.

PART FIVE

There, and Back Again

CHAPTER 24

A Grateful Psychiatrist

When, after so many efforts, you have at last arrived at a certainty,
your joy is one of the greatest that can be felt by a human soul.
—LOUIS PASTEUR (1822–1895)

A
s I was preparing to send this book to the publisher, I had a most wonderful and uplifting experience. A psychiatrist, whom I'll call Dr. Richards, phoned me and said, "I read one of your published articles about chromium in the treatment of depression. I fit your description of patients who respond to chromium to a 'T.' I'd like to make an appointment to come to Chapel Hill and meet with you to find out more about it. Do you have any time?"

I told him I did, and we set up an appointment.

During our first visit, Dr. Richards told me, "I've suffered for much of my adult life from depression. My symptoms are just like the symptoms of the patients you described in your paper who responded to chromium alone in the treatment of depression. My symptoms have been a depressed mood, excess appetite—especially a craving for carbohydrates—excessive sleepiness, unexplained exhaustion, and feeling easily rejected."

Type of Depression: Atypical or Melancholic?

I said to Dr. Richards, "From your brief description of your symptoms, it sounds like you have atypical depression, but to make certain whether you have atypical depression or melancholic depression, we need to go into some detail about your symptoms. May we?"

He answered, "Of course. Please do. But before we start, I must tell you that I don't have a clear idea about the difference between atypical depression and melancholic depression. During my years of training, a distinction between the two was not made."

"I didn't learn about the concept of atypical depression in my psychiatric residency either," I told him. "It's a relatively recent concept. I learned about it just a few years ago in a roundabout way when I was trying to understand what type of depression responds to chromium. As we talk about you, I think the contrast between atypical depression and melancholic depression will become clear."

Onset and Course of Illness

"First let's contrast the onset and course of melancholic depression and atypical depression," I suggested. "Melancholic depression sometimes begins in one's thirties or forties, but often it begins in the fifties or later, the onset is fairly rapid, the change in the person's behavior and functioning are painfully clear to others, and a return to good health often occurs within a few weeks or months. By contrast, atypical depression begins earlier in life, sometimes as early as childhood, and it can last for a lifetime if untreated. In terms of onset and course of illness, melancholic depression is to atypical depression as a summer thunderstorm is to a long, gray winter. Do either of those descriptions fit you?" I asked.

Dr. Richards replied, "The onset of my difficulty fits with atypical depression. I started feeling mildly depressed by the time I was in the fourth or fifth grade."

"As I'm sure you know, people with melancholic depression lose their appetite and taste for food, while people with atypical depression are usually hungry and, in my experience, they crave sweets. What about your appetite?"

Dr. Richards shook his head as if chiding himself and said, "I can't pass a fudge shop without going in. Seems I'm always nibbling. Being hungry and eating too much have been problems for as long as I can remember."

I said, "Hmmm. The arms and legs of many people with atypical depression feel heavy and they have trouble explaining that feeling. That's in contrast to melancholic depression in which a person is agitated, pacing and wringing his or her hands. I don't want to put words in your mouth, but do you feel as if your arms and legs are weighted down?"

Dr. Richards agreed, "You've got it. I've often said I feel like a medieval warrior in a heavy coat of armor, with sheets of metal on my

arms and legs. I'm aware of the phrase 'leaden paralysis' and that certainly describes the sensation in my arms and legs."

I said, "I'm not certain about this, but I think that as depression worsens, so does the feeling of leaden paralysis. Will you comment on that?"

He said, "There is no doubt in my case that the more depressed I feel,
the heavier my arms and legs feel. No doubt."

"OK," I said. "Let's move on to another difference between melancholic and atypical depression, that is, whether your depressed mood is
"frozen," as in melancholic depression, or whether you can feel better
temporarily in response to favorable events in your life, as is the case in
atypical depression."

He responded, "I understand what you're talking about. I've seen
many patients with melancholic depression, and no matter what I or anyone else says or tries to do, they seemed impermeable to influence. My
mood does lift when something good happens to me."

"Being excessively sensitive to rejection and feeling easily deflated is a
symptom of atypical depression," I said. "Are you sensitive to rejection,
and if so, how early in your life did it begin?"

Dr. Richards took a deep breath and sighed before answering. "That's
been a problem for as long as I can remember. I know that my friends and
family love me, and that I'm valued by my colleagues and students, but
despite all the evidence, most of the time I don't believe it. The slightest
indifference by another person seems to nullify the weight of the positive
evidence that people care about me. My feelings are too easily hurt. My
fear that I'll be rejected makes being around people uncomfortable some
of the time."

I continued taking a history. "Some people with atypical depression
are troubled by excessive sleepiness compared to people with melancholic
depression who wake up at three or four in the morning and are unable to
fall back to sleep. Do you have, or have you ever had, a problem with too
much or too little sleep?"

"Over the years I've needed more sleep than most people, and there
are times when I felt like dozing off during the day. But my sleep at night
is not restful."

I summarized, "You have all of the signs of atypical depression,
including early age of onset, excessive appetite, leaden paralysis, excessive
sleepiness, mood reactivity, and sensitivity to rejection. Have you ever
been treated for your difficulty?"

Dr. Richards answered, "Yes. I spent several years in psychoanalysis, which helped me greatly, but it did not relieve my depression. I've tried several antidepressant medications with little benefit and with the usual onerous side effects. I'm taking 20 milligrams per day of Lexapro now. Have been taking it for a year. Hasn't done much for me."

Screening for Insulin Resistance

I told Dr. Richards, "I suspect insulin resistance is a major cause of your depression. I'd like to get a better idea about whether you have insulin resistance by asking about its signs and circumstances associated with it. First, do you tend to gain weight around your abdomen?"

Dr. Richards chuckled, pointed to his large abdomen and said, "Thank you for being polite. We both know the answer to that question. It's obvious I need to lose this potbelly."

"Is your blood pressure high, more than 130 over 85?" I asked.

Dr. Richards answered, "Yes. I take Maxide [an antidiuretic] for it, and it's controlled."

"What about your triglyceride level," I asked. "Is it over 150?"

He shook his head and answered, "No. It was 98 a year ago."

"What about your total cholesterol level?" I asked.

Dr. Richards answered, "It was 211 a year ago and my LDL ['bad'] cholesterol was high at 142."

I continued to ask about other symptoms of atypical depression, "Is your good HDL ['good'] cholesterol less than 40?"

Dr. Richards said, "It was 50 when it was checked a year ago."

"One more question: Is your fasting blood sugar level high, that is, over 100?" I asked.

"No. It's normal."

I asked, "Did any of your close relatives have, or have had, diabetes, heart attack, high blood pressure, or stroke?"

He answered, "No. I don't think so. At least I'm not aware of it."

Insulin Resistance Likely

I told Dr. Richards that a "yes" answer to any one of the questions I had asked him pointed to insulin resistance as a partial cause of his depression, and that he had two of the most telling signs of insulin resistance—abdominal obesity and high blood pressure. "Based on this," I said, "it seems that you may have insulin resistance, and if you do, I think you will respond to chromium."

Dr. Richards, being familiar with the concept, agreed that insulin resistance was a reasonable working assumption, and he queried, "And you think chromium will help with that? But how do you think it works?"

In response, I said to Dr. Richards, "There is much evidence indicating that chromium is an insulin-sensitizing agent. No doubt about that. And it has been demonstrated experimentally that insulin sensitivity is linked to serotonin activity in the brain. My theory—and that's all it is, a theory—is that insensitivity of the body to the action of insulin in some way dampens serotonin activity in the brain. Chromium, by increasing insulin sensitivity, causes an increase in serotonin activity in the brain and that lifts depression, curbs craving for carbohydrates, and restores energy level to normal."

Dr. Richards responded, "Well, that's certainly intriguing and I'm impressed, but skeptical."

I continued by saying, "I can understand why you would be skeptical. So was I at first. But let's take the first step, which is for you to take 800 micrograms of chromium each morning." Dr. Richards asked me if he should discontinue his antidepressant medication. I told him he should continue taking it, at least for a while.

When he asked me which brand of chromium to purchase, I told him that I recommended Chromax chromium picolinate. Near the end of the session, I told Dr. Richards there were at least four more ways, in addition to taking chromium, to decrease insulin resistance and help depression. He said he preferred to wait to discuss them. He wanted to take chromium picolinate alone so he could accurately judge whether or not this one factor would help him.

I told him we could discuss the other modalities later. As the session ended, he thanked me. I asked him to let me know if chromium helped him. He said he was going to be out of the country for a month, but would call when he returned.

Beautiful Results

A month later Dr. Richards called, identified himself, and then left the following exciting message on my answering machine:

"Dr. McLeod, regarding chromium, I've had a very good response to it. Thank you very much for the relief. I feel better than I have felt in over ten years. My symptoms are much down or eliminated. My carbohydrate craving, which was severe before taking chromium, is now minimal. My mood swings have gone away. My depressed mood has gone away. My sense of rejection, which has bothered me for a long time, has greatly lessened. My interest in my usual activities is good. My ability to concentrate is better. I don't feel overwhelmed or anxious and I have good energy.

"Please call me. I want to talk with you about stopping my antidepressant medication. Again, thank you. I'll never be able to thank you enough for what you have done for me."

I was elated. Here again was further proof that chromium had dramatically lifted symptoms of atypical depression. I delightedly played Dr. Richards's message over and over again, and saved it on my answering machine. By now I had seen many people who have had an equally dramatic lifting of depression after beginning chromium. I usually feel good, and always enjoy my work, but hearing of yet another person's success—and being certain it was due to chromium picolinate—made me feel wonderful.

Returning the Call

When I returned Dr. Richards's call, he said, "I'm so grateful to you for your help. Chromium has helped me across the board with all of my symptoms. I wouldn't have believed chromium would help me like this in a hundred years. The only reason I came to see you is because everything else had failed. How long do you think I should take chromium?"

I answered, "For life. Chromium is an essential nutrient. It is safe. In my opinion, it is almost dangerous *not* to take it, not only to prevent depression, but also to prevent other conditions associated with insulin resistance including diabetes, high blood pressure, heart disease, stroke, and in women, infertility due to polycystic ovarian disease. Two recent studies from the Harvard School of Public Health and from Johns Hopkins University showed that chromium deficiency is associated with an increase in heart attacks. Conversely, people with higher levels of chromium were less at risk of having a heart attack.

"In one study conducted by members of the departments of epidemiology and nutrition at Harvard School of Public Health, men with diabetes and heart disease were found to have lower chromium levels than healthy subjects.[1]

"In another study conducted in eight European countries and Israel, Dr. Eliseo Guallar of Johns Hopkins found that lower chromium levels were associated with an increase in the risk of having a heart attack.[2] This risk is especially great in people who are overweight."[3]

Dr. Richards then said, "Do you think that chromium might also be useful in treating bulemic patients? [Bulemic people are those who eat excessively.] I ask that because chromium has such a powerful effect in reducing my carbohydrate craving. It's gone! I'm wondering if I should give chromium to my bulemic patients."

I told Dr. Richards his idea was interesting. I have had two bulemic patients who were helped by chromium, but my experience with this type of patient was limited.

Dr. Richards further asked, "I have another question. Do you think I should stop the antidepressant medication I'm taking? Chromium has helped me so much more."

I said, "Before answering your question, I'd like to review in detail your experience with antidepressant medications."

Dr. Richards answered, "Okay. Several years ago I consulted an expert psychopharmacologist [a psychiatrist who specializes in the use of medications for psychiatric disorders] who prescribed Paxil. I couldn't tolerate it. It dulled me out. My feelings were flat, blunted. I stopped it. Next he prescribed Serzone, but that made me feel funny. So I stopped it too. Next Wellbutrin was prescribed. It was great, but I broke out in a total body rash and had to stop it. About one year ago he prescribed 20 milligrams per day of Lexapro. Despite taking it for over a year now, I'm still depressed and it has made my appetite even more ravenous. My moods continue to swing between mild elation and depression. Before chromium, my moods were like riding a roller coaster, up and down, up and down, up and down."

At this point, I felt confident in offering Dr. Richards a specific recommendation. I said, "Given that you do not think Lexapro has helped you significantly, I advise you to cut the dosage in half and in two weeks stop it altogether. Let's monitor you carefully because we may find that you need both chromium and Lexapro.

"Before we stop talking today, I'd like to discuss with you other ways to improve your insulin functioning, which will protect you against return of depression and improve your general health. While chromium is the mainstay of what I recommend for atypical depression, I also recommend that you lose some weight, exercise, cut down on sweets, potatoes and bread and other starchy carbohydrates, cut down or eliminate saturated and trans fats, and take 2 grams per day of omega-3 fatty acid. Do not take more than 3 grams per day, as large amounts of omega-3 may increase the risk of bleeding in some people."

Dr. Richards said he agreed on the importance of all of these recommendations and said he would adopt all of them.

Dr. Richards and I talked again two weeks after he stopped Lexapro. He said he was doing well without it and "it did very little for me." Three weeks later, however, he called and told me that he had become irritable. I told him that, in my experience, chromium does not help with irritability and that he should resume Lexapro. He did so, and within a week his irritability had lessened. Although chromium is the pillar of Dr. Richards's treatment for depression, he also needed the antidepressant medication, Lexapro.

I asked Dr. Richards how he would compare chromium with the antidepressant medications he has taken. He answered, "There is no comparison. Chromium is far superior. It has helped me across the board with all of my symptoms, except for irritability, and there are no side effects."

Now, six months later, this grateful psychiatrist remains free of depression. He takes 800 micrograms per day of chromium picolinate and 10 milligrams of Lexapro per day.

I asked Dr. Richards if he would ask his family physician to test his blood to see if chromium had had a beneficial effect on his blood lipids (fat). He did so, and was astonished to learn that his total cholesterol had fallen from 211 to 164, his HDL (good) cholesterol had increased from 50 to 60, his triglycerides had fallen dramatically from 98 to 27, and his LDL (bad) cholesterol had fallen from 142 to 98. Dr. Richards was pleased and relieved, but incredulous, so he decided to have his blood tested again. The results were the same.

I asked Dr. Richards if he would give me permission to publish his case history as above. He readily agreed, saying that chromium had helped his depression much more than standard antidepressant medications or psychoanalysis. He said he had practiced psychiatry for all of his adult life and had never seen a treatment as effective for atypical depression as is chromium. He added, "I want to do my part to make this discovery public. Thank you again."

I said that I was pleased too, and told him it was a privilege to be able to work with him. I asked him to stay in touch.

At the End: Looking for the Beginning

My serendipitous discovery that the essential trace element chromium quickly and dramatically relieves atypical depression in many persons is still almost unbelievable to me, even while I continue to see first-hand a cure and hear reports from other psychiatrists of patients who have been helped by taking chromium.

All along as I was reading thousands of articles on chromium, I often saw the name of a Dr. Walter Mertz, one of the early researchers who discovered chromium's essential role in glucose metabolism and insulin functioning in animals. Without his discoveries, I would never have made mine. I wanted to study the research he conducted in the 1950s and 1960s. I was off to the library again.

CHAPTER 25

Where It All Began:
Discovering that Chromium
Is an Essential Ingredient

Every genuine scientist [. . .] is an idealist
in the best sense of the word.

—WILHELM CONRAD RÖNTGEN (1845–1923)

I went to the health sciences library at the UNC Medical School, dusted off old volumes, and found a paper trail that led back to the 1950s. The name of one investigator stood out for his extensive and careful work, Dr. Walter Mertz.

Clearly one of the early preeminent chromium researchers, Mertz had published some 200 articles in scholarly publications such as the *Journal of Biochemistry and Biophysics,* the *American Journal of Physiology,* the *Journal of Biological Chemistry,* and the *Journal of Nutrition.*

The Essential Role of Chromium in Animals

Dr. Mertz and his colleague, Dr. Klaus Schwarz, working at the National Institutes for Health beginning in the 1950s, were trying to find the dietary cause of liver failure in a certain strain of rats. Their work was funded by the Brewer's Yeast Council. Diseases of the liver are associated with excessive alcohol use, especially in the absence of an adequate diet, and the council wanted to understand more about liver failure and how it might be prevented with a change in diet.

Doctors Mertz and Schwarz knew, from the work of others, that a particular strain of rats (Sprague-Dawley) developed impaired glucose metabolism, or glucose intolerance, and liver failure when fed a diet in which torula yeast was the source of protein. *Torula* is the scientific name of a type of yeast that grows on wood. Further, they knew that torula yeast was deficient in at least three substances: the essential amino acid cysteine, vitamin E, and in the mineral element selenium. They suspected that the absence of one of these might be causing the liver failure, and that adding these to the rats' food might prevent liver failure.

In the experiments that followed, all of these elements were added to the rats' food, with the predicted result that liver failure was averted. This was an exciting success, but it left a big question unanswered. The addition of cysteine, vitamin E, and selenium appeared to prevent liver failure, yet the addition of these ingredients did not correct their impaired glucose metabolism.

Drs. Mertz and Dr. Schwarz were puzzled. Until that time, they had assumed that impaired glucose metabolism was an early sign of liver failure, and that both glucose intolerance and liver failure were due to the same dietary deficiencies. Faced with this new evidence, however, the researchers speculated that there was another, as yet unidentified, essential nutrient that was missing from torula yeast. They knew that yeasts vary greatly in their composition of nutrients, depending upon the yeast's source of nutrients. Because torula is deficient in many nutrients, it made sense to replace torula yeast with another natural yeast that had fewer deficiencies.

The doctors selected brewer's yeast, or *Saccharomyces cerevisiae*, and put it into the rats' food. They found that brewer's yeast *did* prevent the development of glucose intolerance. Prior to that time, they thought insulin was the only agent necessary for glucose metabolism. But now they realized that brewer's yeast contained an ingredient that was necessary for insulin to exert its effect on glucose metabolism. They knew their suspect was not insulin as it is not present in brewer's yeast.

They consequently named this unidentified nutritional substance "glucose tolerance factor," or GTF.

Several questions were uppermost in the minds of Dr. Mertz and Dr. Schwarz. The answers to these questions would define some of the properties of GTF. Was the active ingredient soluble in water? Was it destroyed by alcohol? Did it have a positive or negative electrical charge? Was it destroyed by heat or cold? Was it an organic or inorganic compound?

Through a series of experiments, the researchers attempted to isolate the active ingredient of GTF.

Between tests, Dr. Mertz and Dr. Schwarz stored GTF in a refrigerator at almost-freezing temperature (+4° centigrade) and noticed that in some preparations, a brown substance settled to the bottom and adhered to the container.

When the top portion was fed to rats, the animals did not "burn" glucose normally. In other words, the top portion did not contain any GTF activity. The scientists theorized that the cold temperature had destroyed vitamin C or cysteine and that one of these two was the active agent in GTF activity. To test this idea, the researchers added vitamin C and cysteine to the rats' diet. When this did not restore GTF activity, they ruled out both substances. They were still looking for the mystery ingredient.

Doctors Mertz and Schwarz next scraped the brownish substance from the *bottom* of the container and fed it to rats. To their surprise they found that it restored normal glucose metabolism.

To determine whether the brownish substance was an organic or inorganic compound, they exposed it to high temperatures and to a mixture of nitric acid and sulfuric acid ($HNO_3 \bullet H_2SO_4$). This failed to destroy GTF activity, which suggested GTF was an inorganic substance. They further narrowed the list of suspects by determining that the brownish substance had a strong positive electrical charge, so they were able to exclude elements with negative charges. They further narrowed the list of suspects by excluding elements with positive charges that were known to be plentiful in the rats' chow. In this way they identified forty elements that were heat stable, had positive charges, and were not present in the rats' chow. This led them to evaluate a list of forty compounds, from antimony to mercury to zinc.

After six months of many experimental feedings, the two scientists finally determined that only one of the forty elements had any GTF activity. It was chromium.

The next question that Drs. Mertz and Schwarz sought to answer was how chromium exerts its effect on glucose metabolism. From their research, it was clear that both insulin and chromium were involved in glucose metabolism. "Might there be a relationship between the two," they wondered.

To try to answer this question, they gave insulin injections to rats fed chromium-deficient and chromium-rich diets and compared the metabolism of glucose in the two groups. They found that insulin was more efficient in rats that had been fed chromium. In other words, they found that chromium is necessary for insulin to act properly. From this surprising discovery, Dr. Mertz and Dr. Schwarz concluded that chromium is an essential element for normal metabolism in mammals.

I could never do justice to the extensive and careful work of Dr. Mertz and Dr. Schwarz. As I read most of the 200 articles written by Dr. Mertz and his colleagues, I came to admire him as a most careful scientist. I was inspired as I learned how he discovered one nugget of information after another. At times I literally felt a chill and had goose bumps as I read his articles. I wished I had known him.

CHAPTER 26

Our Paths Crossed for a Moment

*To him who devotes his life to science [. . .] his cup of joy is full
when the results of his studies immediately find practical applications.*
—LOUIS PASTEUR (1822–1895)

anting to know more about Dr. Mertz, I found biographical sketches in *American Men and Women of Science* and in *Who's Who in America*. The information stated that Mertz was born May 4, 1923, in Mainz, Germany, and graduated from Mainz Medical School in 1951.

After an internship in surgery and a one-year stint at the University of Frankfurt Hospital, Mertz, then thirty, was awarded a National Institutes of Health (NIH) research fellowship to study liver disease at the Liver Disease Section of NIH. He remained at the Liver Disease Section from 1953 to 1961, when he accepted the position of chief of biological chemistry at Walter Reed Army Institute of Research in Washington, D.C.

In 1969 he was named the chief at the vitamin and mineral nutrition laboratory of the U.S. Department of Agriculture (USDA). From 1969 until he retired in 1993, Dr. Mertz worked as director of Human Nutrition Research of the USDA at the Beltsville Human Nutrition Research Center. Dr. Mertz edited the book *Trace Elements in Human and Animal Nutrition* and was associate editor of the *American Journal of Clinical Nutrition*. He was co-author of the three editions of the authoritative U.S. government's publication "Recommended Dietary Allowances."

Dr. Mertz served at the National Academy of Sciences and was adviser to the "Surgeon General's Report on Nutrition and Health." He had also been recognized with numerous awards, such as the International Prize for Modern Nutrition and the Lederle Award.

I wished I had known Dr. Mertz personally. In his biography at the end of each of his articles, I would notice that he had worked at the National Institute of Arthritis and Metabolic Diseases in Bethesda, Maryland. My mind drifted back to the 1950s, and I recalled where I was when he was making his discoveries. I was an undergraduate, hoping to be accepted into medical school, while Dr. Mertz was beginning his career at NIH. By recalling where I was and where he was, I think I was trying to establish a closeness with him, to find a mentor. I found myself wishing I could ask him about his discoveries and tell him about mine.

I wanted to locate him. I knew that the chances of finding him were slim, but my wish to know him prevailed and I tried nevertheless. To no avail I called the NIH and the information operator in Bethesda. No listing. Next I conducted a nationwide Internet search and found a Walter Mertz in Rockville, Maryland. Could this be the man I was looking for? I called the number. A woman answered, and I asked for Dr. Walter Mertz. She said, "Just a moment, please." It was a tense moment for me. I so much wanted to speak with him but I was intimidated by his splendid accomplishments. A man said, "Hello." I introduced myself and asked if this was the Dr. Mertz who had done research in chromium. "Yes," he answered. "That was a long time ago." My heart jumped. I stammered some and told him how thrilled and inspired I had been while reading his work. I told him I had discovered the role of chromium in mood regulation, had written articles on the topic, and was now writing a book about the discoveries. I said that I was writing a chapter about him and his discoveries. Dr. Mertz asked me to send him reprints of my articles and the chapter, which I did.

Within a few days, Dr. Mertz replied, "Congratulations on your discovery of the role of chromium in the treatment of depression. It comes as a complete surprise to me. I am enclosing a review I wrote more than thirty years ago. This is the last copy, which I have saved for the person who would extend my own research into an entirely new field. It is yours."

With gratitude, I framed his letter and review article and hung them in my office, where they will remain as long as I am in practice.

Dr. Mertz and I exchanged several letters, emails, and phone calls, clarifying points about his research and career. I asked if I could visit him and discuss our discoveries in person; he seemed enthusiastic. I suggested that we meet on Sunday, June 2, 2002. Dr. Mertz hesitated and said, "I will be sick then. Let's tentatively plan to meet on Sunday, June 9. Please call on Wednesday, June 5, to confirm."

The predictability of illness saddened me and alerted me to the probability that he was receiving chemotherapy for cancer. This proved to be the case and our plan to meet was again thrown into question when I called on Wednesday and Mrs. Mertz said, "Dr. Mertz wants to see you, but this is not a good time. He is very ill. He is receiving chemotherapy. Please call back on Friday, after he has seen his doctor, to see if he will be able to meet with you on Sunday."

I called on Friday, but there was no answer. I feared the worst. I imagined he was hospitalized, or worse—dead. I called the next day, and reached his answering machine. I left a message that I was sorry he was ill, that I certainly did not want to intrude, but if he would like me to visit him the following day, I would. I had resigned myself to never meeting him. I attempted to console myself with the awareness that I had indeed met a soulmate in science, a fellow explorer. I hoped, and believed, he was pleased that his discoveries were being extended into a new field.

Unexpectedly on Saturday night, Dr. Mertz left three messages on my answering machine indicating how very much he wanted me to visit him. He acknowledged the visit would have to be brief and apologized for calling late. I telephoned to confirm and left for Maryland in the wee hours of the morning. For me it was a pilgrimage, and I was happy to be on the road. I arrived in his neighborhood at 10:00 A.M. The day was warm and beautiful. A couple was strolling a baby.

Face to Face

I arrived at the Mertz neighborhood, a green, tranquil suburb, a sharp contrast to the busy interstate highway just a few miles away. His home was modest; a well-manicured lawn and pansies lined the walkway. A decade-old Honda sat in the driveway. When Mrs. Mertz greeted me, I thanked her for inviting me and promised I'd stay only a short time. Dr. Mertz followed a moment later. Both were quite welcoming and grateful that I had traveled so far on short notice to see him. He invited me to sit in his family room. The window looked out onto a wooded backyard.

As we sat down, I wondered what lay behind his deep eyes. "What had been his sorrows? His joys?" But that was too personal. I told myself to limit our conversation to science. I started our talk by showing Dr. Mertz the framed letter and review article he had sent me. I told him they would hang in my office as long as I was in practice. He smiled and called for Mrs. Mertz and proudly showed them to her. Next I asked about some details that were not clear in his papers, as well as some questions I had about his professional career. After being with him a few minutes, I realized he was a modest, warm, and deeply committed man, someone more in love with science than with himself. When I complimented him on one of his discoveries, he gave partial credit to others and said, "In science, each of us does his little part. We're part of a bigger fabric. We advance the work of others."

I was curious about how Mertz came to work at the NIH, and he told me the pertinent details about his career in medicine, and especially his longtime research interest in diabetes and insulin's mechanism of action. During medical school, he had wanted to interrupt his clinical studies to do three months of research in this area but had been denied permission.

He recalled, "You wouldn't believe the atmosphere in German medical schools when I was a student. The professor knew everything. He was like the Pope, infallible. I'm not exaggerating. Their attitude was that everything had been discovered. Research was almost viewed as insubordination."

Only three months after his initial request had been turned down, however, Dr. Mertz was recruited to come to the United States as a research fellow by a man he had known in medical school, Dr. Klaus Schwarz. Dr. Schwarz had immigrated to the United States in 1948 and had become chief of the liver disease section of the National Institute of Arthritis and Metabolic Diseases.

Dr. Mertz continued, "The atmosphere at NIH was dramatically different from that in Germany. Scientists were guaranteed absolute freedom to do research at NIH, and the atmosphere was highly collegial. You're not going to believe this." Then Dr. Mertz leaned forward toward me, his eyes twinkling and he exclaimed, "The second day I was at NIH, I received a call from the great Nobel laureate, Dr. Bernardo Houssay [an Argentinean endocrinologist who discovered that the anterior pituitary gland in the brain plays a role in blood sugar regulation]. He said he had heard I was interested in endocrinology and asked me what my thoughts were about his research, what I agreed with and disagreed with, and what direction I thought future research should take. Can you imagine that, a Nobel laureate asking me, a beginner, what I thought of his work?"

With obvious admiration, Dr. Mertz went on, "The NIH was—and still is today—the finest research facility in the world."

I was savoring the conversation, and Dr. Mertz seemed to be enjoying it as well, but I became concerned when he coughed deeply. Might I be exhausting him? I asked if he felt well enough to continue. He said he was enjoying our talk and wanted to continue. A few moments later, Mrs. Mertz came in and asked the same question. He answered, "I'm enjoying this, my dear. If I must get tired, I can't think of a better way to tire myself out than by talking about these discoveries."

Returning to the topic of research: I commented that great discoveries are often greeted with great disbelief and asked Dr. Mertz if his discovery—that chromium is an essential trace mineral—was met with much doubt.

His response, "Oh, yes. Klaus [Schwarz] didn't believe it, and I didn't believe it either. At that time, chromium was known only as a very toxic heavy metal. We just followed the evidence and tried to rid ourselves of this preconceived idea. Years of research were required to overcome this prejudice and recognize that chromium exists in many forms, some of which are toxic, but one of which is essential for human metabolism."

I reminded Dr. Mertz that the misconception has not been totally dispelled. The late-1990s' movie, *Erin Brockovich,* stirred fears that chromium is always dangerous. The movie did not make it clear that chromium exists in many forms.

He nodded his head and stated, "Yes. There are many forms of chromium. Chromium-6, or hexavalent chromium, is an industrial form that is toxic. Nutritional chromium is safe."

Dr. Mertz asked me to tell him how I discovered the role of chromium in mood regulation. I gave him a brief summary and promised to send him book chapters describing my findings in detail.

He also wanted to know if chromium alone is effective or whether only a combination of chromium and an antidepressant relieves depression. "Both are true," I answered. "Some people require a combination of chromium picolinate and an antidepressant medication, while some others require only chromium." To illustrate the latter point, I briefly described Joseph's response to chromium alone.

Dr. Mertz was obviously pleased and commented, "This has such enormous potential to relieve the suffering of millions of people. Your discovery reminds me of the discovery of the essential role of other trace elements, such as iron and iodine."

His words, "relieve the suffering of millions," had a distinctive inflection and echoed in my mind as words imbued with deeper meaning. But I quickly returned to science. "Aren't you surprised," I asked, "by the profound effects that chromium has on so many systems of the human body?"

He answered, "Yes and no. In medical school, the expression was, 'If you understand insulin, you understand the entire body.' It seems plausible when one understands that insulin affects so many bodily functions and chromium is necessary for insulin to work effectively. When viewed in that light, it is understandable."

Then Dr. Mertz asked me if there were any new studies published on chromium's effect on the cardiovascular system? I told him about a recently published article concerning a study conducted at Harvard School of Public Health and Johns Hopkins that showed that low levels of chromium increase a person's risk of a heart attack. Dr. Mertz said that the result made sense, given the close association between impaired glucose metabolism and cardiovascular disease.

Then Dr. Mertz returned to the question that seemed to fascinate him most. "Is anyone investigating the mechanism whereby chromium regulates mood? This type of research is so important. I hope your work will stimulate research in that direction."

I told him about research conducted by Jirí Horácek: a physician from the Czech Republic that demonstrated a relationship between glucose metabolism and serotonergic activity in the brain. It was logical to hypothesize a mechanism of action in which chromium enables insulin to work properly and insulin in turn increases brain serotonin (a chemical messenger that regulates mood). I also mentioned that a group in Oxford, England, led by Professor Phil Cowen, was conducting basic research on chromium's effect on the central nervous system. This obviously delighted Dr. Mertz, who smiled.

He offered the following thought, "I have been thinking a lot about your work, especially as [far as] the mode of action is concerned. Do you believe that the old insulin shock therapy of half a century ago, when it worked, might have worked not *via* the resulting hypoglycemia but through a different mechanism? If attacks of depression are caused by ineffective insulin, the situation could be remedied for a short time by massive doses of the hormone (insulin), or in the long run by chromium."

"Very, very interesting," I answered. "I'll think about that." And I have.

Farewells

At the end of our meeting, I thanked Dr. Mertz for seeing me and answering my questions, and I asked if he had any questions for me.

He paused, looked reflectively upward, and said, "No. No questions. But there is something I want to tell you. I have lung cancer. The diagnosis was made six months ago. It is a slow-growing tumor. I'm satisfied with my chemotherapist. I've always tried to see the positive side of things, and the positive side of this is that I know I won't die from some dreaded disease like Alzheimer's or Parkinson's disease. There are worse ways to go."

I was moved and inspired by his serenity and said to him, "You must have been loved deeply to have that degree of optimism and strength."

He answered, "Yes, I was. Most definitely." And then, again, Dr. Mertz turned to the topic that fascinated him most and said, "I don't know how much time I have left, but I plan to spend all of my available energy thinking about possible mechanisms of action for chromium in depression. I thank you for giving me a new goal, a new inspiration, and for coming to see me. I will send you any ideas I have, and I'd like you to do the same."

I promised I would and got up to leave. Dr. Mertz walked with me and stood on the front porch and waved farewell, as I waved back.

As I was driving away, I was trying to be as brave as Dr. Mertz. Two Biblical phrases that I thought described him well kept running through my mind: "Love with all of thy heart and all of thy strength" (Deuteronomy 6:5) and "Well done, good and faithful servant" (Matthew 25:21).

Dr. Mertz died at home on Friday, June 28, 2002.

CHAPTER 27

Putting It All Together

We [now] devote more attention to the patient's diet and habits,
and more often send him away with good advice [rather]
than with hastily written prescriptions.

—ROBERT HALL BABCOCK (1851–1917), *physician who recognized the*
importance of diet in the treatment and prevention of disease

Now that we've journeyed together through most of the book, at this point, I want to offer some practical, actionable steps you can take. Before you take the steps, though, first ask yourself the following two questions.

Question 1: Do You Have Atypical Depression?

If you're down, blue, or discouraged, please answer the next five questions:

- Do you crave sweets and other carbohydrates or tend to gain weight, especially around your abdomen?

- Are you tired for no obvious reason, or do your arms and legs feel heavy, as if made of lead?

- Do you tend to nod off or to be excessively sleepy?

- Are your feelings easily hurt by rejection from others?

- Did your depression begin before age thirty?

If you answered "yes" to one or more of the five questions above, you may have atypical depression.

Question 2: Is Your Depression Caused by Insulin Resistance?

If your atypical depression is caused in part by insulin resistance, it probably will respond to chromium picolinate. To determine if you might have insulin resistance, please answer the following questions:

- Do any of your blood relatives have or have any of them had or experienced diabetes, heart attack, high blood pressure, or stroke?

- Do you tend to gain weight around your abdomen?

- Is your blood pressure high, more than 130 over 85?

- Is your triglyceride level high, over 150?

- Is your fasting blood sugar level high, over 100?

- Is your good (HDL) cholesterol less than 35 (for women) or 40 (for men)?

- For women: Did you have diabetes during pregnancy?

If you're like most people in that you don't know what the specific numbers are in your laboratory tests, I suggest you obtain the results from a laboratory test done within the last six months or, lacking that, obtain a new blood test from your family physician.

Even *one* yes answer to *any one* of the questions above suggests your depression might be caused in part by insulin resistance. Making this assumption based on only one yes answer may result in a false-positive diagnosis of insulin resistance, but I would rather be wrong and early than correct and late. Prevention is so much easier than treatment. Moreover, the treatment I recommend is benign and important for overall good health.

Ways to Improve Insulin Functioning

If your atypical depression is based on insulin resistance, I recommend that you do the following steps:

- Take chromium picolinate

- Lose weight

- Reduce simple sugars, and saturated and trans fats in your diet

- Supplement your diet with omega-3 fatty acids

- Exercise regularly

1 Take Chromium Picolinate

Taking chromium picolinate is the mainstay of my treatment plan. Without it, people with atypical depression may find it impossible to improve insulin functioning and relieve depression.

Chromium picolinate will improve your body's sensitivity to the action of insulin. The result is that the "feel-good" chemical in your brain called serotonin will most likely increase, thus relieving your depression, carbohydrate craving, and exhaustion, and also making you less sensitive to rejection.

I recommend that you take between 400 to 1,000 micrograms of chromium daily in the form of chromium picolinate to help the action of insulin in your body. Why this form of chromium? Chromium picolinate is the most easily absorbed form of supplemental chromium. The proper dosage to take is approximately 4 micrograms per pound of body weight per day. For example, a person weighing 150 pounds should take 600 micrograms of chromium picolinate per day; for someone weighing 200 pounds, 800 micrograms per day.

This recommended dosage, however, varies according to the individual patient—not only body weight, but also other factors such as severity of symptoms will determine the best dosage for you. Although chromium picolinate is very safe, to be on the safe side, I never recommend taking more than 1,000 micrograms per day.

What brand of chromium picolinate should you use? I typically recommend Chromax chromium picolinate made by Nutrition 21 in Purchase, New York. The company's telephone number is 1-866-CHROMAX (1-866-247-6629) and the website address is www.chromax.com.

2 Lose Weight

If you are overweight, I recommend losing excess weight. Doing so improves the sensitivity of the body to insulin. Being overweight does not cause insulin resistance, but it certainly makes it worse, as fat requires larger amounts of insulin to keep glucose in a normal range.[1]

3 Reduce the Amount of Sweets, Starchy Carbohydrates, and Saturated and Trans Fats in Your Diet

Sweets, candy, and most soft drinks contain sugar in its simplest form, which goes almost directly into the bloodstream and needs few intermediate steps to be transformed into glucose. Eating sweets causes insulin spikes and eventually impairs insulin functioning.[2-3] Starchy carbohydrates such as bread, pasta, white rice, and potatoes are rapidly absorbed and also cause insulin spikes.

Insulin spikes lead to hunger, which leads to eating yet more calories and gaining more weight. The pancreas eventually gets overworked so that it does not function well to produce enough insulin, thus causing a severe form of insulin resistance, which is type 2 diabetes.

An easy rule of thumb to keep in mind is this, "If it is white or sweet, don't eat it, except occasionally." Of course, there are exceptions such as cauliflower, egg whites, fish, and other seafood.

Reducing the amount of simple carbohydrates is especially necessary for those who are sensitive to carbohydrates in general. How do you know if your body has trouble handling carbohydrates? If you feel hungry or shaky an hour or two after eating carbohydrates—for example, pancakes with maple syrup or a large, rich dessert—your body may be especially sensitive to carbohydrates and therefore all the more reason to avoid or reduce the amount of sweets and starchy carbohydrates in your diet.

One of the editors who reviewed this book wrote, "An aside: I have memories from age five to ten of eating our traditional Sunday breakfast of pancakes and waffles and within thirty minutes sliding into depression and an awful overall feeling." That particular editor's depression was relieved by taking Chromax chromium picolinate.

Not all carbohydrates are "bad," however. The human body needs carbohydrates, but the "good" kind—complex carbohydrates, such as those found in many vegetables—don't cause insulin spikes. The reason is that they take longer to be broken down into glucose in the bloodstream, which allows the pancreas to secrete insulin slowly.

It is also important that you reduce the amount of saturated fat and trans fatty acids in your diet, as these two types of fat increase insulin levels and worsen insulin resistance.[4] They also lead to an increase in the risk of heart attack and stroke. Saturated fats are those fats found in beef, pork, butter, and other animal and dairy products. Trans fatty acids are found in mostly fried foods, baked goods (cookies, crackers), and margarine.

The human body needs some fat to repair cells and quell appetite. Unless we eat some fat, we never feel full. "Good" fat comes in two forms, monounsaturated and polyunsaturated. Monounsaturated fat is the type found in olive oil, canola oil, nuts, and seeds. Polyunsaturated fat is found in corn, safflower, and sunflower oils. But remember, "good" fat can make you fat, as it is packed with calories. A tablespoon of olive oil contains as many calories as a scoop of ice cream.

There is another type of fat that the body needs known as omega-3 fatty acids.

4 Take an Omega-3 Fatty Acid Supplement

Omega-3 fatty acid is one of the two main classes of polyunsaturated fats; the other is called omega-6 fatty acids. Both are essential fatty acids, meaning that they are essential to the proper functioning of the body and cannot be made by the body, so they must be acquired from the diet. For optimal health, a diet should contain equal amounts of omega-3 and omega-6 fatty acids.

The modern Western diet is abundant in omega-6 as it is found in oils made from vegetables and seeds such as safflower, sunflower, olive and corn. However, omega-3 acids, which are found mainly in oily fish, are lacking. Not only does the modern diet in the developed world not contain much fish, but also some species of fish have been found to have levels of contamination with mercury and cancer-causing toxins. Where a fish is caught and what food a farm-raised fish is fed compounds the problem.

Omega-3 fatty acids are necessary for the normal development and functioning of the brain. They are also beneficial for a healthy heart. In addition, two scientific studies showed evidence that omega-3 fatty acids may have an antidepressant and mood-stabilizing effect, and another study showed that when omega-3 fatty acids were added to the diet of insulin-resistant rats that had previously been fed a high-fat diet, insulin resistance was reversed.[5–7]

If you are depressed, I recommend that you take 3 grams per day of omega-3 fatty acids or fish oil (sometimes labeled "fish body oils"). More than 3 grams per day may increase the risk of bleeding in some people. After your depression lifts, I recommend that you take a maintenance dosage of 1 gram a day.

What brand of omega-3 should you take? As with all dietary supplements, minerals, and herbs, one must be careful what brand to choose. To select a good omega-3 supplement, check the label to see if it states that the capsule of fish oil contains at least 50 percent, or preferably more, of omega-3 fatty acids. Then cut the capsule open and smell it. If it's rank, throw it away and find another supplement.

I have found that the best brand of omega-3 is called OmegaBrite because it contains the highest concentration of omega-3 in the capsules and is manufactured under rigorous scientific standards. It is made by Omega Natural Science in Waltham, Massachusetts. The company's telephone number is 1-800-383-2030, and the website is www.omegabrite.com.

5 Exercise

Exercise that increases the body's use of oxygen (aerobic exercise) and resistance exercise (such as weight lifting or using machines) helps lower insulin resistance—both at the time one is exercising and over the long term—by contributing to weight loss. Results of a study carried out in the late 1980s by M.A. Rogers, M.D. and colleagues in the Department of Medicine at the Washington University School of Medicine in St. Louis, Missouri, showed people with mild impairment of glucose metabolism who exercised vigorously decreased their insulin resistance, and thus improved the "burning" of glucose in their bodies.[8]

Before recommending an exercise routine, however, I advise you to have a thorough physical examination by your family doctor. I cannot stress this more strongly. After getting a clean bill of health from your physician, I encourage you to seek a competent physical fitness trainer to teach you how to exercise properly and how to minimize the risk of injury.

If your doctor determines that your heart is healthy, I recommend some form of aerobic exercise at least thirty minutes a day, four or five times a week. Overly strenuous exercise is not necessary—in fact, it can be injurious. A brisk walk or swimming laps can fit the bill for many people. If there is some evidence from your doctor that you have a heart problem, I encourage you to develop some type of exercise program in collaboration with a cardiologist.

Other Steps You May Wish to Try

Treatment with Psychoanalysis or Insight-oriented Psychotherapy

Although there is no objective evidence per se that either psychoanalysis or insight-oriented psychotherapy relieves insulin resistance directly, I recommend this form of treatment in conjunction with the other strategies listed above. "Talk therapy" can help you understand why you may not be acting in your best interest. For example, you may be overeating for many reasons including loneliness, boredom—even defiance. Getting to the root of these reasons can be the first step in becoming open to the recommendations I have made, as well as uncovering some of the roots of your depression and any other emotional difficulties you may have.

Possible Use of Medication to Help Lower Insulin Resistance

In spite of conscientiously and continuously following all recommendations to improve or lower insulin resistance, you may require the help of medication for that particular purpose. Each person's body and mind is entirely individual and can react differently to many factors, both internal and external. You should not feel inadequate should medication for insulin resistance be necessary.

Some antidepressant medications, and some medications for diabetes, reduce insulin resistance. I only prescribe antidepressant medications for some people with insulin resistance whose condition has not yielded positive results to the recommendations above. However, for those patients who require medication for type 2 diabetes—a severe form of insulin resistance—I send them to their family doctor, because prescribing for a serious, non-psychiatric medical condition is outside my domain.

Conclusion

By following all the recommendations above, you probably will be able to increase your body's sensitivity to insulin and lift your depression. Not only your depression, but your general overall health is very likely to be improved as well. Feeling as if we have a new lease on life—and a better, more enjoyable life—begins with you, your friend, or your loved one.

I hope that chromium picolinate—and the other measures I recommend—will help you as much as it helped George, Elizabeth, Sara, Joseph, the grateful psychiatrist, and many other fine people whom I've been privileged to treat.

With all best wishes . . .

Appendices

APPENDIX A: GEORGE'S SCL-90 SELF-RATING SCALE SEVEN DAYS BEFORE CHROMIUM SUPPLEMENTATION

NAME: *George*

DATE: *5-9-XX*

SYMPTOM CHECKLIST 90 (SCL-90)

Enter a number to the right of each question in the column indicating how much you have been bothered by each symptom.

0 = Not at all; 1 = Mild; 2 = Moderate; 3 = Severe; 4 = Extreme

	0	1	2	3	4
1. Headaches				3	
2. Nervousness or shakiness inside	0				
3. Unwanted thoughts, words, or ideas that won't leave your mind	0				
4. Faintness	0				
5. Loss of sexual pleasure or interest			2		
6. Feeling critical of others			2		
7. The idea that someone else can control your thoughts	0				
8. Feeling others are to blame for most of your troubles	0				
9. Trouble remembering things				3	
10. Worried about sloppiness or carelessness	0				
11. Feeling easily annoyed or irritated			2		
12. Pains in heart or chest	0				
13. Feeling afraid in open spaces or on the streets	0				
14. Feeling low in energy or slowed down					4
15. Thoughts of ending your life	0				
16. Hearing voices that other people do not hear	0				
17. Trembling	0				

(Self-Rating Scale continued)	0	1	2	3	4
18. Feeling that most people cannot be trusted	O				
19. Poor appetite	O				
20. Crying easily	O				
21. Feeling shy or uneasy with the opposite sex	O				
22. Feeling of being trapped or caught	O				
23. Suddenly scared for no reason	O				
24. Temper outbursts that you could not control		1			
25. Feeling afraid to go out of your house alone	O				
26. Blaming yourself for things	O				
27. Pains in lower back	O				
28. Feeling blocked in getting things done		1			
29. Feeling lonely	O				
30. Feeling blue		1			
31. Worrying too much about things	O				
32. Feeling no interest in things				3	
33. Feeling fearful	O				
34. Your feelings are easily hurt	O				
35. Other people being aware of your private thoughts	O				
36. Feeling others do not understand or are unsympathetic	O				
37. Feeling that people are unfriendly or dislike you	O				
38. Having to do things very slowly to insure correctness	O				
39. Heart pounding or racing	O				
40. Nausea or upset stomach	O				
41. Feeling inferior to others	O				
42. Soreness of your muscles			2		
43. Feeling that you are watched or talked about by others	O				
44. Trouble falling asleep	O				

(Self-Rating Scale continued)	0	1	2	3	4
45. Having to check and double-check what you do	O				
46. Difficulty making decisions			2		
47. Feeling afraid to travel on buses, subways, trains, or airplanes	O				
48. Trouble getting your breath	O				
49. Hot or cold spells	O				
50. Having to avoid certain things, places, or activities because they frighten you	O				
51. Your mind going blank			2		
52. Numbness or tingling in parts of your body	O				
53. A lump in your throat	O				
54. Feeling hopeless about the future	O				
55. Trouble concentrating			2		
56. Feeling weak in parts of your body				3	
57. Feeling tense or keyed up		1			
58. Heavy feelings in your arms or legs			2		
59. Thoughts of death or dying	O				
60. Overeating				3	
61. Feeling uneasy when people are watching or talking about you	O				
62. Having thoughts that are not your own	O				
63. Having urges to beat, injure, or harm someone	O				
64. Awakening in the early morning	O				
65. Having to repeat the same actions such as touching, counting, washing	O				
66. Sleep that is restless or disturbed				3	
67. Having urges to break or smash things	O				
68. Having ideas or beliefs that others do not share	O				

(Self-Rating Scale continued)	0	1	2	3	4
69. Feeling very self-conscious with others	O				
70. Feeling uneasy in crowds, such as shopping or at a movie	O				
71. Feeling everything is an effort			2		
72. Spells of terror or panic	O				
73. Feeling uncomfortable about eating or drinking in public	O				
74. Getting into frequent arguments	O				
75. Feeling nervous when you are left alone	O				
76. Others not giving you proper credit for your achievements	O				
77. Feeling lonely even when you are with people	O				
78. Feeling so restless you can't sit still	O				
79. Feelings of worthlessness	O				
80. Feeling that familiar things are strange or unreal	O				
81. Shouting or throwing things		1			
82. Feeling afraid you will faint in public	O				
83. Feeling that people will take advantage of you if you let them	O				
84. Having thoughts about sex that bother you a lot	O				
85. The idea that you should be punished for your sins	O				
86. Feeling pushed to get things done	O				
87. The idea that something serious is wrong with your body	O				
88. Never feeling close to another person	O				
89. Feelings of guilt	O				
90. The idea that something is wrong with your mind	O				

To graphically illustrate how dramatic George's improvement was, the reader is invited to compare the before and after SCL-90 (to follow), as well as a graph of the comparison on page 190.

APPENDIX B: GEORGE'S SCL-90 SELF-RATING SCALE FIVE DAYS AFTER CHROMIUM SUPPLEMENTATION

NAME: *George*

DATE: *5-16-XX*

SYMPTOM CHECKLIST 90 (SCL-90)

Enter a number to the right of each question in the column indicating how much you have been bothered by each symptom.

0 = Not at all; 1 = Mild; 2 = Moderate; 3 = Severe; 4 = Extreme

	0	1	2	3	4
1. Headaches	O				
2. Nervousness or shakiness inside	O				
3. Unwanted thoughts, words, or ideas that won't leave your mind	O				
4. Faintness	O				
5. Loss of sexual pleasure or interest	O				
6. Feeling critical of others	O				
7. The idea that someone else can control your thoughts	O				
8. Feeling others are to blame for most of your troubles	O				
9. Trouble remembering things		1			
10. Worried about sloppiness or carelessness	O				
11. Feeling easily annoyed or irritated	O				
12. Pains in heart or chest	O				
13. Feeling afraid in open spaces or on the streets	O				
14. Feeling low in energy or slowed down		1			
15. Thoughts of ending your life	O				
16. Hearing voices that other people do not hear	O				
17. Trembling	O				

(Self-Rating Scale continued)	0	1	2	3	4
18. Feeling that most people cannot be trusted	O				
19. Poor appetite	O				
20. Crying easily	O				
21. Feeling shy or uneasy with the opposite sex	O				
22. Feeling of being trapped or caught	O				
23. Suddenly scared for no reason	O				
24. Temper outbursts that you could not control	O				
25. Feeling afraid to go out of your house alone	O				
26. Blaming yourself for things	O				
27. Pains in lower back	O				
28. Feeling blocked in getting things done	O				
29. Feeling lonely	O				
30. Feeling blue	O				
31. Worrying too much about things	O				
32. Feeling no interest in things	O				
33. Feeling fearful	O				
34. Your feelings are easily hurt	O				
35. Other people being aware of your private thoughts	O				
36. Feeling others do not understand or are unsympathetic	O				
37. Feeling that people are unfriendly or dislike you	O				
38. Having to do things very slowly to insure correctness	O				
39. Heart pounding or racing	O				
40. Nausea or upset stomach	O				
41. Feeling inferior to others	O				
42. Soreness of your muscles	O				
43. Feeling that you are watched or talked about by others	O				
44. Trouble falling asleep	O				

(Self-Rating Scale continued)	0	1	2	3	4
45. Having to check and double-check what you do	O				
46. Difficulty making decisions	O				
47. Feeling afraid to travel on buses, subways, trains, or airplanes	O				
48. Trouble getting your breath	O				
49. Hot or cold spells	O				
50. Having to avoid certain things, places, or activities because they frighten you	O				
51. Your mind going blank	O				
52. Numbness or tingling in parts of your body	O				
53. A lump in your throat	O				
54. Feeling hopeless about the future	O				
55. Trouble concentrating	O				
56. Feeling weak in parts of your body		1			
57. Feeling tense or keyed up	O				
58. Heavy feelings in your arms or legs	O				
59. Thoughts of death or dying	O				
60. Overeating	O				
61. Feeling uneasy when people are watching or talking about you	O				
62. Having thoughts that are not your own	O				
63. Having urges to beat, injure, or harm someone	O				
64. Awakening in the early morning	O				
65. Having to repeat the same actions such as touching, counting, washing	O				
66. Sleep that is restless or disturbed	O				
67. Having urges to break or smash things	O				
68. Having ideas or beliefs that others do not share	O				

(Self-Rating Scale continued)	0	1	2	3	4
69. Feeling very self-conscious with others	O				
70. Feeling uneasy in crowds, such as shopping or at a movie	O				
71. Feeling everything is an effort	O				
72. Spells of terror or panic	O				
73. Feeling uncomfortable about eating or drinking in public	O				
74. Getting into frequent arguments	O				
75. Feeling nervous when you are left alone	O				
76. Others not giving you proper credit for your achievements	O				
77. Feeling lonely even when you are with people	O				
78. Feeling so restless you can't sit still	O				
79. Feelings of worthlessness	O				
80. Feeling that familiar things are strange or unreal	O				
81. Shouting or throwing things	O				
82. Feeling afraid you will faint in public	O				
83. Feeling that people will take advantage of you if you let them	O				
84. Having thoughts about sex that bother you a lot	O				
85. The idea that you should be punished for your sins	O				
86. Feeling pushed to get things done	O				
87. The idea that something serious is wrong with your body	O				
88. Never feeling close to another person	O				
89. Feelings of guilt	O				
90. The idea that something is wrong with your mind	O				

APPENDIX C:
■ GEORGE'S SYMPTOMS BEFORE CHROMIUM SUPPLEMENTATION
■ GEORGE'S SYMPTOMS AFTER CHROMIUM SUPPLEMENTATION

0 = Not at all; 1 = Mild; 2 = Moderate; 3 = Severe; 4 = Extreme

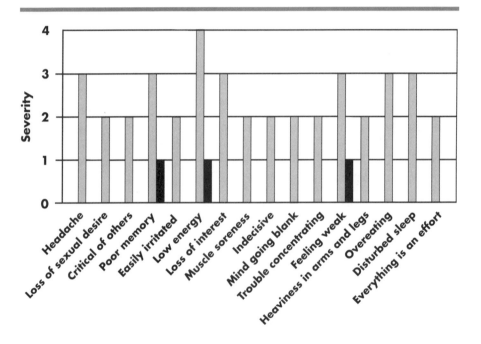

Symptoms: The only symptoms listed are those George rated moderate, severe, or extreme before beginning chromium.

Glossary

Clinical Global Improvement (CGI). This self-rating scale measures overall improvement. The scales ask the participant to rate their feelings ranging from "very much improvement" (rating = 1) to "very little or none" (rating = 7).

Columbia Atypical Depression Diagnostic Scale (ADDS). This interview is designed to determine whether key atypical symptoms are present and, if so, how severe they are. The symptoms are sensitivity to rejection, temporary lifting of depressed mood in response to changes in the environment, increased appetite, increased weight gain, increased sleep, and feelings of tiredness and fatigue.

Dietary Supplement. A product that is added to the diet and contains one or more of the following ingredients: a vitamin, mineral, amino acid, herb, or other botanicals. They are incorporated in capsule form, tablets, powder, extracts, liquids, or gel caps. They can be found in grocery stores, natural food stores, and over the Internet.

Hamilton Depression Scale (HAM-D). A 29-item, interview-based scale rates the key symptoms of depression, including low mood, feelings of guilt, thoughts of suicide, disturbed sleep patterns, increase in appetite, weight gain, and decrease in energy.

Mini-International Neuropsychiatric Interview (MINI). This is a standard interview with specific questions to identify a series of probable disorders, including depression.

Symptom Checklist 90 (SCL-90). This is a 90-item self-rating scale covering a wide range of symptoms including depression, anxiety, hostility, and rejection sensitivity. (*See* Appendices A and B.)

Symptom Occurrence Scale (SOS). This 34-item, self-rating scale rates symptoms from none (0) to severe (3). Many of these symptoms can occur from drug treatment and are considered to be treatment side effects if they worsen relative to their level before treatment.

Internet Resources

Here are some resources, both for consumers and healthcare practitioners, for additional information:

ARTICLES FOR CONSUMERS

"Ask the Doctor: What Are the Symptoms of Atypical Depression?"
http://www.depression.org/NNewsFolder/v25/v25md1.html

"Atypical Depression"
http://www.healthyplace.com/communities/depression/atypical.asp

"Atypical Depression"
http://www.mcmanweb.com/article-200.htm

"Atypical Depression Actually Very Typical" by Nancy Schimelpfening
http://depression.about.com/cs/diagnosis/a/atypicaldepress.htm

"Atypical Depression: The Symptoms" by John McManamy
http://www.dbsalliance.org/research/ResearchUpdate12.html

"Atypical Depression: Thyroid Link Still Alive" by Daniel DeNoon
http://my.webmd.com/content/article/83/97918.htm

"The Many Faces of Depression" by Hara Estroff Marano
http://cms.psychologytoday.com/articles/pto-20030806-000015.html

"Types of Major Depression: Depression with Atypical Features"
http://holistic-online.com/Remedies/Depression/dep_types_atypical.htm

ARTICLES FOR HEALTHCARE PRACTITIONERS

"Atypical Depression"
http://www.gpnotebook.co.uk/simplepage.cfm?ID=235274315

"Atypical Depression"
http://www.fpnotebook.com/PSY59.htm

"Atypical Depression: Clinical Aspects and Noradrenergic Function"
by G.M. Asnis, L.K. McGinn and W.C. Sanderson
http://www.biopsychiatry.com/atypnor.htm

"Atypical Depression: Piecing Together Symptoms, Treatments"
by Erik B. Nelson, M.D.
http://www.currentpsychiatry.com/2003_04/0403_depression.asp

"Chromium Picolinate Supplementation Linked with Reduced
Carbohydrate Cravings Associated with Atypical Depression"
http://www.docguide.com/news/content.nsf/news/8525697700573E188525
6EA70066FAFC?OpenDocument&c=Depression&count=10&id=48DDE4
A73E09A969852568880078C249

"Chromium Picolinate Supplementation Reduced Carbohydrate Cravings
and Atypical Depression"
http://www.news-medical.net/?id=2140

"Identification of Atypical Depression with Atypical Features"
http://www.findarticles.com/p/articles/mi_m3225/is_4_69/ai_112915243

"A Reappraisal of Atypical Depression"
by Frederic M. Quitkin, M.D., Patrick J. McGrath, M.D.,
Jonathan W. Stewart, M.D., and Donald F. Klein, M.D.
http://ajp.psychiatryonline.org/cgi/content/full/160/4/798-b

"Study Shows Psychotherapy As Effective As Drug Therapy
for Atypical Depression"
http://www.pslgroup.com/dg/fdb32.htm

"The Symptoms of Atypical Depression" (Letters to the Editor)
http://www.cpa-apc.org/Publications/Archives/CJP/2003
/june/lettersSymptoms.asp

"Treatment Recommendations for Patients with Major Depressive Disorder"
http://www.psych.org/psych_pract/treatg/pg/Depression2e.book-9.cfm

MENTAL HEALTH ORGANIZATIONS

Anxiety Disorders Association of America
http://www.adaa.org

Canadian Mental Health Association
http://www.cmha.ca/english

Depression and Bipolar Support Alliance (DBSA)
http://www.dbsalliance.org

Depression and Related Affective Disorders Association (DRADA)
http://www.drada.org

Families for Depression Awareness
http://www.familyaware.org

Mental Health Council of Australia
http://www.mhca.com.au

Mental Health Europe
http://www.mhe-sme.org/en/home.htm

The Mental Health Foundation (U.K.)
http://www.mentalhealth.org.uk

Mental Health Ireland
http://www.mentalhealthireland.ie/default.asp

National Alliance for the Mentally Ill (NAMI)
http://www.nami.org

Stress, Anxiety & Depression Resource Center
http://www.stress-anxiety-depression.org/depression

Suicide and Mental Health Association International
http://suicideandmentalhealthassociationinternational.org

World Federation for Mental Health (WFMH)
http://www.wfmh.org

CRISIS CENTERS

National Hopeline Network (Kristin Brooks Hope Center)
http://www.hopeline.com
phone: 1-800-SUICIDE (1-800-784-2433)

PreventSuicideNow.com
http://preventsuicidenow.com
phone: 1-800-SUICIDE (1-800-784-2433)

Suicide Prevention Action Network
http://www.spanusa.org
phone: 1-800-273-TALK (1-800-273-8255)

QUALITY SOURCES FOR SUPPLEMENTS MENTIONED IN THIS BOOK

For chromium picolinate:

- Chromax Chromium Picolinate
  1-866-CHROMAX (1-866-247-6629) or www.chromax.com

- Solgar Chromium Picolinate
  1-800-223-1216 or www.vitaminshoppe.com

- VitaminWorld Chromium Picolinate
  1-800-228-4533 or www.vitaminworld.com

For omega-3 fatty acids:

- Omega Natural Science's OmegaBrite (gel caps)
  1-800-383-2030 or www.omegabrite_gelcap.html

- Solgar MaxEPA Softgels (1,000 mg)
  1-800-223-1216 or www.vitaminshoppe.com

- Vitamin Shoppe EPA-DHA Omega-3 Fish Oil (softgels)
  1-800-223-1216 or vitaminshoppe.com

References

CHAPTER 2

1. Williamson DE, Birmaher B, Brent DA, et al. "Atypical symptoms of depression in a sample of depressed child and adolescent outpatients." *J Am Acad Child Adolesc Psychiatry,* 2000; 39(10):1253–1259.

2. Matza LS, Revicki DA, Davidson JRT, et al. "Depression with atypical features in the national comorbidity survey: classification, description, and consequences." *Arch Gen Psychiatry,* 2003; 60:817–826.

3. Benazzi F. "Can only reversed vegetative symptoms define atypical depression?" *Eur Arch Psychiatry Clin Neurosci,* 2002; 252(6):288–293.

4. West ED, Dally PJ. "Effects of iproniazid in depressive syndrome." *Br Med J,* 1959; 1:1491–1494.

5. Posternak MA, Zimmerman M. "Partial validation of the atypical features subtype of major depressive disorder." *Arch Gen Psychiatry* 2002; 59(1):70–76.

6. Davidson JR, Miller R, Turnbull CD, et al. "Atypical depression." *Arch Gen Psychiatry,* 1982; 39:527–534.

7. Derecho CN, Wetzler S, McGinn LK, et al. "Atypical depression among psychiatric inpatients: clinical features and personality traits." *J Affect Disord,* 1996; 39(1):55–59.

8. Alpert JE, Uebelacker LA, McLean NE, et al. "Social phobia, avoidant personality disorder and atypical depression: co-occurrence and clinical implications." *Psychol Med,* 1997; 27(3):627–633.

9. See notes 2–3.

10. Nierenberg AA, Alpert JE, Pava J, et al. "Course and treatment of atypical depression." *J Clin Psychiatry,* 1998; 59 (suppl 18):5–9.

11. Loomer HP, Saunders JC, Kline NS. "A clinical and pharmacodynamic eval-

uation of iproniazid as a psychic energizer." *Psychiatr Res Rep Am Psychiatr Assoc,* 1957; 8:129–141.

CHAPTER 3

1. Bowlby J. *Attachment and Loss. Vol. 1, Attachment.* New York: Basic Books, 1969.

2. Bowlby J. *Attachment and Loss. Vol. 2, Separation: Anxiety and Anger.* New York: Basic Books, 1973.

3. Bowlby J. *Attachment and Loss: Vol. 3, Loss.* New York: Basic Books, 1980.

4. Kendler KS, Neale MC, Kessler RC, et al. "A longitudinal twin study of 1-year prevalence of major depression in women." *Arch Gen Psychiatry,* 1993; 50(11):843–852.

5. Lyons MJ, Eisen SA, Goldberg J, et al. "A registry-based twin study of depression in men." *Arch Gen Psychiatry,* 1999; 56(1):39–44.

6. Preuss UW, Schuckit MA, Smith TL, et al. "A comparison of alcohol-induced and independent depression in alcoholics with histories of suicide attempts." *J Stud Alcohol,* 2002; 63(4):498–502.

7. Nurnberger J, Foroud T, Flury L, et al. "Evidence for a locus on chromosome 1 that influences vulnerability to alcoholism and affective disorder." *Am J Psych,* 2001; 158:718–724.

CHAPTER 4

1. Babyak MA, Blumenthal JA, Herman S, et al. "Exercise treatment for major depression: maintenance of therapeutic benefit at 10 months." *Psychosomatic Medicine,* 2000; 62: 633–638.

2. Blumenthal JA, Babyak MA, Moore KA, et al. "Effects of exercise training on older patients with major depression." *Arch Internal Med,* 1999; 159:2349–2356.

3. Stoll AL. *The Omega-3 Connection: The Groundbreaking Antidepression Diet and Brain Program.* New York: Simon and Schuster, 2001.

4. Stoll AL, Severus WE, Freeman MP, et al. "Omega 3 fatty acids in bipolar disorder: a preliminary double-blind, placebo-controlled trial." *Arch Gen Psychiatry,* 1999; 56(5):407–412.

5. Klerman GL, Weissman MM. "Increasing rates of depression." *JAMA,* 1989; 261: 2229–2235.

6. Quitkin FM, Rifkin A, Klein DF. "Monoamine oxidase inhibitors: a review of antidepressant effectiveness." *Arch Gen Psychiatry,* 1979; 36:749–760.

7. Davidson J, Raft D, Pelton S. "An outpatient evaluation of phenelzine and imipramine." *J Clin Psychiatry,* 1987; 48:143–146.

8. Liebowitz MR, Quitkin FM, Stewart JW, et al. "Antidepressant specificity in atypical depression." *Arch Gen Psychiatry,* 1988; 45:129–137.

9. Quitkin FM, Stewart JW, McGrath PJ, et al. "Phenelzine versus imipramine in the treatment of probable atypical depression: defining syndrome boundaries of selective MAOI responders." *Am J Psychiatry,* 1988; 145:306–311.

10. Quitkin FM, Harrison W, Stewart JW, et al. "Response to phenelzine and imipramine in placebo nonresponders with atypical depression: a new application of the crossover design." *Arch Gen Psychiatry,* 1991; 48:319–323.

11. McGrath PJ, Stewart JW, Janal MN, et al. "A placebo-controlled study of fluoxetine versus imipramine in the acute treatment of atypical depression." *Am J Psychiatry,* 2000; 157:344–350.

CHAPTER 7

1. Quitkin FM, Stewart JW, McGrath PJ, et al. "Phenelzine versus imipranine in the treatment of probable atypical depression: defining syndrome boundaries of selective MAOI responders." *Am J Psychiatry,* 1988; 145:306–311.

2. Quitkin FM, Stewart JW, Mc Grath PJ, et al. "Columbia atypical depression: a subgroup of depressives with better response to MAOI than to tricyclic antidepressant or placebo." *Br J Psychiatry,* 1993;163(suppl 21):30–34.

3. McGrath PJ, Stewart JW, Janal MN, et al. "A placebo-controlled study of fluoxetine versus imipramine in the acute treatment of atypical depression." *Am J Psychiatry,* 2000; 157(3):344–350.

4. Joyce PR, Mulder RT, McKenzie JM, et al. "Atypical depression, atypical temperament and a differential antidepressant response to fluoxetine and nortriptyline." *Depress Anxiety,* 2004; 19(3):180–186.

5. Joyce PR, Mulder RT, Luty SE, et al. "Patterns and predictors of remission, response and recovery in major depression treated with fluoxetine or nortriptyline." *Aust NZ J Psychiatry,* 2002; 36(3):384–391.

6. Pande AC, Birkett M, Fechner-Bates S, et al. "Fluoxetine versus phenelzine in atypical depression." *Biol Psychiatry,*1996; 40(10): 1017–1020.

7. Sogaard J, Lane R, Latimer P, et al. "A 12-week study comparing moclobemide and sertralinee in the treatment of outpatients with atypical depression." *J Psychopharmacol,* 1999;13(4):406–414.

CHAPTER 8

1. Sternbach H. "The serotonin syndrome." *Am J Psychiatry,* 1991; 148: 705–713.

2. Brown TM, Skop BP, Mareth TR. "Pathophysiology and management of the serotonin syndrome." *Ann Pharmacother,* 1996; 30:527–533.

3. Lane R, Baldwin D. "Selective serotonin reuptake inhibitor-induced serotonin syndrome: review." *J Clin Psychopharmacol,* 1997; 17:208–221.

CHAPTER 10

1. Shils ME, Olson JA, Shike M, eds. *Modern Nutrition in Health and Disease.* 8th ed. Philadelphia, PA: Lea & Febiger, 1994.

2. National Institutes of Health (NIH) Office of Dietary Supplements http://ods. od.nih.gov/.

3. Benton, D., Cook, R. "Selenium supplementation improves mood in a double-blind crossover trial." *Psychopharmacology [Berl],* 1990; 102:549–550.

CHAPTER 12

1. Coppen A. "The biochemistry of affective disorders." *Br J Psychiatry,* 1967; 113(504):1237–1264.

2. Anderson GH, Li ET, Glanville NT. "Brain mechanisms and the quantitative and qualitative aspects of food intake." *Brain Res Bull,* 1984; 12(2):167–173.

3. Møller SE. "Serotonin, carbohydrates, and atypical depression." *Pharmacol Toxicol,* 1992; 71(suppl 1):61–71.

4. Smith S, Sauder C. "Food cravings, depression, and premenstrual problems." *Psychosom Med,* 1969; 31:281–287.

5. Fernstrom D, et al. "Diurnal variations in plasma concentrations of tryptophan, tryosine, and other neutral amino acids: effect of dietary protein intake." *Am J Clin Nutr,* 1979; 32:1912–1922.

6. Wurtman JJ, et al. "Effect of nutrient intake on premenstrual depression." *J Obstet Gynecol,* 1989; 161:1228–1234.

7. Both-Orthman B. "Menstrual cycle phase-related changes in appetite in patients with premenstrual syndrome and in control subjects." *Am J Psychiatry,* 1988; 145:628–631.

8. Krauchi K, Wire-Justice A, Graw P. "The relationship of affective state to dietary preference: winter depression and light therapy as a model." *I Affect Disord,* 1990; 20:43–53.

9. Lieberman HR, Wurtman J, Chew B. "Changes in mood after carbohydrate consumption among obese individuals." *Am J Clin Nutr,* 1986; 45:772–778.

10. Brzezinski A, Wurtman JJ, Wurtman RJ, et al. "d-Fenfluramine suppresses the increased calorie and carbohydrate intakes and improves the mood of women with premenstrual syndrome." *Obstet Gynecol,* 1990; 76:296–301.

11. Jermain DM, Preece CK, Sykes RL, et al. "Luteal phase sertraline treatment for premenstrual dysphoric disorder: results of a double-blind, placebo-controlled, crossover study." *Arch Fam Med,* 1999; 8(4):328–332.

12. Freeman EW, Rickels K, Sonheimer SJ. "Sertraline versus desipramine in the treatment of premenstrual syndrome: an open-label trial." *J Clin Psychiatry*, 1996; 57:7–11.

13. Ozeren S, Corakci A, Yucesoy I, et al. "Fluoxetine in the treatment of premenstrual syndrome." *Eur J Obstet Gynecol Reprod Biol*, 1997; 73(2):167–170.

14. Yonkers KA, Halbreich U, Freeman E, et al. "Symptomatic improvement of premenstrual dysphoric disorder with sertraline treatment: a randomized controlled trial." *JAMA*, 1997; 278:983–988.

15. Steiner M, Steinberg S, Stewart D, et al. "Fluoxetine in the treatment of premenstrual dysphoria." *NEJM*, 1995; 332:1529–1534.

16. Menkes DB, Coates DC, Fawcett JP. "Acute tryptophan depletion aggravates premenstrual syndrome." *J Affect Disord*, 1994; 32(1):37–44.

17. Ehrenkranz JR. "Effects of sex steroids on serotonin uptake in blood platelets." *Acta Endocrinologica*, 1976; 83:420–428.

18. Taylor DL, Mathew RJ, Ho BT, et al. "Serotonin levels and platelet uptake during premenstrual tension." *Neuropsychobiology*, 1984; 12:16–18.

19. Ashby CR Jr, Carr LA, Cook CL, et al. "Inhibition of serotonin uptake in rat brain synaptosomes by plasma from patients with premenstrual syndrome." *Biol Psychiatry;* 1992; 31(11):1169–1171.

20. Ashby CR Jr, Carr LA, Cook CL, et al. "Alteration of 5-HT uptake by plasma fractions in the premenstrual syndrome." *J Neural Transm*, 1990; 79(1–2):41–50.

CHAPTER 13

1. Nielsen FN. Chromium. In *Modern Nutrition in Health and Disease*, Vol. 1, 8th ed, edited by ME Shils, JA Olson, M Shike. Philadelphia, PA: Lea & Febiger, 1994.

2. Janus JA, Krajnc EI. Integrated criteria document chromium: effects. Appendix. Bilthoven, Netherlands: National Institute of Public Health and Environmental Protection, 1990.

3. Smyth HF, Carpenter CP, Weil CS, et al. "Range-finding toxicity data: list VII." *Am Ind Hyg Assoc J*, 1969; 30: 470–476.

4. Ivankovic S, Preussmann R. "Absence of toxic and carcinogenic effects after administration of high doses of chromic oxide pigment in subacute and long-term feeding experiments in rats." *Food Cosmet Toxicol*, 1975; 13:347–351.

5. Mertz W, Abernathy CO, Olin SS. *Risk Assessment of Essential Elements.* Washington, DC: ILSI Press, 1994.

6. Stearns DM, Wise JP Sr, Patierno SR, et al. "Chromium (III) picolinate produces chromosome damage in Chinese hamster ovary cells." *FASEB Journal*, 1995; 9:1643–1649.

7. Anderson RA, Bryden NA, Polansky MM. "Lack of toxicity of chromium chloride and chromium picolinate in rats." *J Am Coll Nutr,* 1997; 16:273–279.

8. Slesinki RS, Gudi R, San R, et al. "Chromium picolinate does not produce chromosome damage in the in vitro mammalian chromosome aberration test with CHO cells." *Environmental and Molecular Mutagenesis,* 2004; 44(3): 208.

9. Slesinki RS, San R, Clarke J, et al. "Lack of mutagenicity of chromium picolinate in the CHO/HGPRT mutation assay: Results from standard tests and a test with a 48-hour exposure period." *Environmental and Molecular Mutagenesis,* 2004; 44(3): 227.

10. Schwartz K, Mertz W. "Chromium (III) and the glucose tolerance factor." *Arch Biochem Biophys,* 1959; 85:292–295.

11. Schroeder HA. "Chromium deficiency in rats: a syndrome simulating diabetes mellitus with retarded growth." *J Nutr,* 1966; 88:439–445.

12. Mertz W. "Chromium in human nutrition: a review." *J Nutr,* 1993; 123: 626–633.

13. Schroeder HA, Nason AP, Tipton IH. "Chromium deficiency as a factor in atherosclerosis." *J Chronic Dis,* 1970; 23:123–142.

14. Hambridge KM. "Chromium nutrition in man." *Am J Clin Nutr,* 1974; 27:505–514.

15. Newman HA, Leighton RF, Lanese RR, et al. "Serum chromium and angiographically determined coronary artery disease." *Clinical Chemistry,* 1978; 24:541–544.

16. Riales R, Albrink MJ. "Effect of chromium chloride supplementation on glucose tolerance and serum lipids including high-density lipoprotein of adult men." *Am J Clin Nutr,* 1981; 34:2670–2678.

17. Schroeder HA, Vinton WH, Balassa JJ. "Effects of chromium, cadmium, and lead on the growth and survival of mice." *J Nutr,* 1963; 80:48–54.

18. Anderson RA, Plansky MM. "Dietary chromium deficiency: effect on sperm count and fertility in rats." *Biol Trace Elem Res,* 1981; 3:1–5.

19. Evans GW, Meyer LK. "Life span is increased in rats supplemented with a chromium-pyridine 2 carboxylate complex." *Adv in Sci Res,* 1994; 1:19–23.

CHAPTER 16

1. Schwarz K. Mertz W. "A glucose tolerance factor and its differentiation from factor 3." *Arch Biochem Biophys,* 1957; 72:515–518.

2. Schwarz K, Mertz W. "Chromium (III) and the glucose tolerance factor." *Arch Biochem Biophys,* 1959; 85:292–295.

3. Mertz W, Roginski EE. "The effect of trivalent chromium on galactose entry in rat epididymal fat tissue." *J Biol Chem,* 1963; 238:868–872.

4. Mertz W, Thurman DE. "Chromium in newborn rats." *Fed Proc,* 1968; 27:482 (abstract).

5. Mertz W, Roginski, EE. "Effects of chromium (III) supplementation of growth and survival under stress in rats fed low protein diets." *J Nutr,* 1969; 97:531–536.

6. Jeejeebhoy KN, Chu RC, Marliss EB, et al. "Chromium deficiency, glucose intolerance, and neuropathy reversed by chromium supplementation, in a patient receiving long-term total parenteral nutrition." *Am J Clin Nutr,* 1977; *30: 531–538.*

7. Hopkins LL Jr, Ransome-Kuti O, Majaj AS. "Improvement of impaired car- bohydrate metabolism by chromium (III) in malnourished infants." *Am J Clin Nutr,* 1968; 21:203–211.

8. Gurson CT, Saner G. "Effect of chromium on glucose utilization in marasmic protein-calorie malnutrition." *Am J Clin Nutr,* 1971; 24:1313–1319.

9. Levine RA, Streeten DHP, Doisy RJ. "The effect of trivalent chromium on glucose tolerance in elderly human subjects." *Metabolism, 1968;* 17:114–125.

10. Freund H, Atamian S, Fischer JE. "Chromium deficiency during total par- enteral nutrition." *JAMA,* 1979; 241:496–498.

11. Borel JS, Majerust TC, Polansky MM, et al. "Chromium intake and urinary chromium excretion of trauma patients." *J. Biol. Trace Elem Res,* 1984; 6:317–326.

12. Brown RO, Forloines-Lynn S, Cross, Heizer WD. "Chromium deficiency after long-term parenteral nutrition." *Dig Dis Sci,* 1986; 31;661–664.

13. Anderson RA. Recent advances in the clinical and biochemical effects of chromium deficiency. In *Essential and Toxic Trace Elements in Human Health and Disease,* edited by AS Prasad. New York: Wiley Liss, 1993.

14. Anderson RA. "Chromium and parenteral nutrition." *Nutrition, 1995;* 11:83–86.

CHAPTER 17

1. Reaven GM. 1988. Banting Lecture: Role of insulin resistance in human dis- ease. *Diabetes,* 1988; 37:1595–607.

2. _____. Syndrome X: 6 years later. *J Intern Med Suppl,* 1994; 736:13–22.

3. Zavaroni I, Mazza S, Dall'Aglio E, et al. "Prevalence of hyperinsulinaemia in patients with high blood pressure." *J Intern Med* 1992; 231:235–240.

4. McLaughlin T, Abbasi, F, Cheal K, et al. "Use of metabolic markers to iden- tify overweight individuals who are insulin resistant." *Ann Intern Med,* 2003; 802–809.

CHAPTER 18

1. Heidema ST. "Blutzuckerbestimmugen bei psychiatrischen und neurologischen Patienten. *Ztschr. f. d. ges.*" *Neurol. u. Psychiat,* 1919; 48:111–129.

2. Wuth O. "Der Blutzucker bei Psychosen Allg." *Ztschr. f. Psychiat,* 1920–1921; 76: 817–818.

3. Kooy FH. "Hyperglycaemia in mental disorders." *Brain,* 1919–1920; 42:214–289.

4. Drury KK, Farran-Ridge C. "Some observations on the types of blood-sugar curve found in different forms of insanity." *Jour Ment Sci,* 1925; 71:8–29.

5. Mann, SA. "Blood-sugar studies in mental disorders." *J Ment Sci,* 1925;. 72:443–473.

6. Banting FG. 1925. Nobel Lecture: "Diabetes and insulin." 1925.

7. MacLeod JJR. 1925. Nobel Lecture: "The physiology of insulin and its source in the animal body."

8. McCowan PK, Quastel JH. "Blood-sugar studies in abnormal mental states." *Lancet,* 1931; 221:731–736.

9. McFarland RA, Goldstein H. "The biochemistry of manic-depressive psychosis: a review." *Am J Psychiat,* 1939; 96:21–58.

10. Pryce IG. "Melancholia, glucose tolerance, and body weight." *J Ment Sci,* 1958; 104:421–442.

11. ———. "The relationship between glucose tolerance, body weight, and clinical state of melancholia." *J Ment Sci,* 1958; 104:1079–1090.

12. Soeldner JS, Slore D. "Critical variables in the radioimmunoassay of serum insulin using the double antibody technic." *Diabetes,* 1965; 14:771–779.

13. Mueller PS, Heninger GR, McDonald RK. "Intravenous glucose tolerance test in depression." *Arch Gen Psychiatry,* 1969; 21:470–477.

14. Wright JH, Jacisin JJ, Radin NS, et al. "Glucose metabolism in unipolar depression." *Br J Psychiatry,* 1978; 132:386–393.

15. Potter van Loon BJP, Radder JK, Frolich M, et al. "Fluoxetine increases insulin action in obese nondiabetic and in obese non-insulin-dependent diabetic individuals." *Int J Obes Relat Metab Disord,* 1992; 16:79–85.

16. Winokur A, Maislin G, Phillips JL, et al. "Insulin resistance after oral glucose testing in patients with major depression." *Am J Psychiatry,* 1988; 3:325–330.

17. Eaton WW, Armenian H, Gallo J, et al. "Depression and risk for onset of type II diabetes: a prospective, population-based study." *Diabetes Care,* 1996; 19:1097–1102.

18. Kawakami NN, Takatsuka N, Shimizu H, et al. "Depressive symptoms and occurrence of type 2 diabetes among Japanese men." *Diabetes Care, 1999; 22:1071–1076.*

CHAPTER 19

1. McLeod MN, Gaynes BN, Golden RN. "Chromium potentiation of antidepressant pharmacology for dysthymic disorder in 5 patients." *Journal of Clinical Psychiatry*, 1999; 60:237-240.

2. *Psychiatry Drug Alerts*, June 1999:13.

3. *Review Series: Psychiatry*, 2000: 2:16–17.

CHAPTER 21

1. Lepkifker E, Dannon PN, Iancu I, et al. "Nightmares related to fluoxetine treatment." *Clin Neuropharmacol*, 1995:18, 90–94.

2. McLeod MN, Gaynes BN, Golden RN. "Chromium potentiation of antidepressant pharmacotherapy for dysthymic disorder in 5 patients." *J Clin Psychiatry*, 1999; 60:237–240.

3. Blundell JE. "Is there a role for serotonin (5-hydroxytryptamine) in feeding?" *Int J Obes*, 1977; 1:15–42.

4. Blundell JE. Serotonin and Feeding. In *Serotonin in Health and Disease*. Vol. 5, Clinical Applications, edited by WB Essman. New York: Spectrum, 1979.

5. Blundell JE. "Serotonin and appetite." *Neuropharmacology*, 1984; 23(128): 1537–1551.

CHAPTER 22

1. McLeod MN, Golden RN. "Chromium treatment of depression." *International Journal of Neuropsychopharmacology*, 2000; 3:311–314.

CHAPTER 23

1. Davidson JRT, Abraham K, Connor KM, McLeod MN. "Effectiveness of chromium in atypical depression: a placebo-controlled trial." *Biological Psychiatry*, 2003; 53: 261–264.

CHAPTER 24

1. Pajpathak S, Rimm EB, Li T, et al. "Levels of chromium in toenails and the risk of cardiovascular disease in diabetic men." *Circulation*, 2004; 109(7): P119

2. Guallar E, Jimenez J, van t' Veer P, et al. "The association of chromium with the risk of a first myocardial infaction in men." The EURAMIC Study [abstract]. *Circulation*. 2001; 103:1366.

3. Rimm EB, Guallar E, Giovannucci E, et al. "Toenail chromium levels and risk of coronary heart disease among normal and overweight men." American Heart Association's 42nd Annual Conference on Cardiovascular Disease, Epidemiology, and Prevention, Honolulu, Hawaii, April 24, 2002.

CHAPTER 27

1. Storlien L, Else P, Edwell F, et al. Dietary fats, obesity and insulin resistance. In *Progress in Obesity Research, 8th ed.* edited by G Ailhaud and B Guy-Grand. London, England: John Libbey & Co., 1998.

2. Storlien LH, Kraegen EW, Jenkins AB, et al. "Effects of sucrose vs. starch diets on in vivo insulin action, thermogenesis, and obesity in rats." *Am J Clin Nutr*, 1988; 47:420–427.

3. Thorburn AW, Storlien LH, Jenkins AB, et al. "Fructose-induced in vivo insulin resistance and elevated plasma triglyceride levels in rats." *Am J Clin Nutr*, 1989; 49:1155–1163.

4. Storlin LH, Higgins JA, Thomas TC, et al. "Diet composition and insulin action in animal models." *Br J Nutr*, 2000; 83:S85–S90.

5. Stoll AL, Severus WE, Freeman MP, et al. "Omega-3 fatty acids in bipolar disorder: a preliminary double-blind, placebo-controlled trial." *Arch Gen Psychiatry*, 1999; 56(5):407–412.

6. Nemets B, Ziva-Stahl Z, Belmaker RH. "Addition of omega-3 fatty acid to maintenance medication treatment for recurrent unipolar depressive disorder." *Am J Psychiatry*, 2002; 159:477-479.

7. Storlien LH, Kraegen EW, Chisholm DJ, et al. "Fish oil prevents insulin resistance induced by high-fat feeding in rats." *Science*, 1987; 237(4817): 885–888.

8. Rogers MA. "Acute effects of exercise on glucose tolerance in non-insulin-dependent diabetes." *Med Sci Sports Exerc*, 1989; 21:362–368.

Index

Abraham, Kurian, 143
Abuse
  physical, 16, 79, 81
  sexual, 16, 81, 82, 113
Alcoholism, 14, 17, 26–27, 129
Anderson, Richard, 71–72
Antidepressants, 21–22, 46, 54, 105,
  135, 137, 138, 141, 159, 179.
  See also Monoamine oxide
  inhibitors (MAOIs); Selective
  serotonin reuptake inhibitors
  (SSRIs); Tricyclics.
Appetite, 8–9, 58, 62, 81, 122, 125,
  135, 141, 154
Atypical depression, 4–12, 126
  causes, 13–17
  onset, 8, 154
  symptoms, 4, 8–10, 64, 125,
  153–161, 173
  treatment, 19–22, 53–55, 57–58,
  60, 121, 132–139

Banting, Frederick, 102
Benefit/risk ratio, 68–69, 72–73
Bernard, Claude, 138
Blood pressure, 12
  high, 95, 128, 131, 156
Blood sugar. *See* Glucose.

Brewer's yeast, 163
Buchwald, Art, 20
Bulimia, 159
Burton, Robert, 127

Caffeine, 48
Cancer, 71, 72
Carbohydrates, 21, 63, 97, 140, 159,
  175, 176
Case histories
  Al, 99–100
  Alice, 111–115
  Dr. Richards, 153–161
  Elaine, 109–111
  Elizabeth, 61–65
  George, 3–7, 14–18, 23–33,
  37–38, 44–45, 50–60, 137–138,
  182–190
  Jackson, 118–119
  Jim, 115–118
  Joseph, 123–139, 141–142
  Mary, 119–121
  Sara, 74–86
Chelation, 48, 49
Childhood loss, 16, 79
Cholesterol, 160
  HDL, 95, 156, 160
  LDL, 156, 160

triglycerides, 96, 156, 160
Chromax, 157, 175
Chromium, 67, 89–92, 94, 105,
    163–165, 170
    dosage, 59–60, 72, 175
    general benefits, 72, 158
    hexavalent, 67, 170
    picolinate, 49–50, 53–55, 56, 57,
        59, 64, 67, 84–86, 110–111,
        117, 118, 119, 120–121,
        132–139, 141–142, 149–150,
        157–160, 174, 175
    response time, 53, 57, 117,
        133–134, 150
    safety, 66–73
    side effects, 150
    trivalent, 67, 69
Churchill, Winston, 20
Clinical Global Improvement (CGI),
    148, 191
Color perception, 135
Columbia Atypical Depression Scale
    (ADDS), 147, 148, 191
Committee on Mutagenicity (COM),
    72
Connor, Katharine, 143
Cowen, Phil, 171

Dally, P. J., 10
Danish, Nabila, 143–144, 147, 148
Davidson, Jonathan R. T., 141, 142,
    143–145, 148–149
Dependence, 27, 120
Depression, 4, 24, 99–105
    causes, 13–17, 99
    See also Atypical depression;
        Endogenous depression;
        Melancholic depression.
Diabetes, 15, 55–56, 99, 104–105
    type 2, 96, 97, 105, 111, 129,
        141, 176, 179

Diet, 21, 159–160, 175–178
Dietary supplements, 191
Disappointment, fear of, 27
Dreams, 53, 57–58, 114, 117, 118,
    122, 134–135, 137
Drugs, illegal, 14
Duke University Medical Center.
    Institutional Review Board
    (IRB), 144–145

Eating disorders, 82. See also
    Bulimia.
Eaton, William, 105
Elavil, 113, 128
Endogenous depression, 103
Ephedra, 43, 48
Erin Brockovich (movie), 67, 170
Essential nutrients, 90, 158,
    162–165
Exercise, 20–21, 159, 174, 178
Exhaustion, 3, 9, 100, 125, 141,
    154–155

Fats, 160, 174, 175, 176–177
Fish, 177
    oil, 21, 177
Freud, Sigmund, 29, 41
Freund, Herbert, 91–92
Fruit, 132
Fugue state, 82

Genetics, 17
Ginseng, 48, 56
Glucose, 55, 89–92, 94, 96, 97,
    100–102, 156
    intolerance, 56, 96, 99–104, 131,
        162–165
Golden, Robert, 45, 46, 51, 54, 56,
    57, 121, 135, 141–145
Grief, 76–79
Guallar, Eliseo, 158
Guarana, 48, 55–56

Hamilton Depression Scale (HAM–D), 148, 149, 191
Heart disease, 141, 158–159, 171
Horácek, Jirí, 171
Hunger, excessive. See Appetite.
Hyperinsulinemia, 95

Insulin, 49, 63, 64, 90, 91, 94–96, 97, 102, 131, 132, 171, 174–175, 176
   receptors, 94–95, 131
   resistance, 93, 95–98, 103, 104, 111, 131–132, 139, 156–157, 174, 177–179
   sensitivity, 104, 139, 142, 157
Iproniazid, 11, 12
Irritability, 160
Ivankovic, Stanislav, 70

Jeejeebhoy, Khursheed, 90–91, 92

Kava, 43, 48
Kawakami, Norito, 105

Leaden paralysis, 125, 155
Lexapro, 156, 159, 160
Lincoln, Abraham, 20
Lithium, 83

Ma huang. See Ephedra.
Macleod, J. J. R., 102
Manganese, 50
Mania, 38–39
Mann, S. A., 101–102
Masochism, moral, 117
McNamara, James O., 143
Medical conditions, 13–14
Medications, 12, 14
Melancholic depression, 8, 10, 124, 154
Mertz, Walter, 91, 161, 162–172
   biography, 166–167
Minerals, 48–49

Mini-International Neuropsychiatric Interview (MINI), 147, 191
Modern Nutrition in Health and Disease, 49, 66–67
Molybdenum, 50
Monoamine oxide, 11
Monoamine oxide inhibitors (MAOIs), 11, 12
   side effects, 12, 31
Mood reactivity, 9
Morgan, John, 45
Mueller, Peter, 103

National Institutes of Health (NIH), 169–170
   Office of Dietary Supplements, 49
Nielsen, Forrest H., 66
Nierenberg, Andrew A., 10
Nutrition, 21, 139, 143, 144, 175

Obesity, 96
   trunkal, 95, 131, 156
Obsessive compulsive disorder (OCD), 83
Occam's razor, 128
Omega–3 fatty acids, 160, 174, 177–178
Omega–6 fatty acids, 177
OmegaBrite, 178

Pamelor, 113
Panic attacks, 119, 127
Paxil, 83
Picolinates, 48
Placebo response, 39–41, 52
Pre-diabetes. See Glucose, intolerance.
Premenstrual syndrome (PMS), 62, 64, 83–84, 85, 110, 111, 122
Preussmann, Rudolph, 70
Principle of parsimony. See Occam's razor.

Proust, Marcel, 136
Prozac, 63, 104, 110, 119
Pryce, I. G., 103
Psychotherapy, 19–20, 22, 23–25, 80,
    115, 116, 121, 129, 178–179

Quackery, 42–43

Rejection, 28, 29
Responsibility, delegation of, 27
Rogers, M. A., 178
Roosevelt, Eleanor, 20

SAD. See Seasonal affective disorder
    (SAD).
Schwartz, Klaus, 162, 169, 170
Seasonal affective disorder (SAD),
    141
Selective serotonin reuptake
    inhibitors (SSRIs), 21, 32, 64
    side effects, 32, 33
Selenium, 49, 56
Sensitivity, 9, 28, 29, 124, 155
Serotonin, 60, 62, 64, 135, 157, 171,
    175
    syndrome, 39, 110
Sleep, 9, 155
Smyth, Henry F., 69–70
Social phobia, 9, 127
Solzhenitsyn, Alexander, 40
St. John's wort, 48
Stearns, Diane, 71, 72
Stress, 15
Styron, William, 20
Sugar. See Sweets.
Suicide, 7
Sweets, 21, 97, 159, 174, 175
    craving for, 62–63, 81, 97, 100,
        125, 154
Symptom Check List 90 (SCL–90),
    50–51, 53, 54, 63, 64, 148,
    182–189, 191

Symptom Occurrence Scale (SOS),
    148, 192

Talk therapy. See Psychotherapy.
Therapeutic alliance, 28
Tofranil, 120
Total parenteral nutrition (TPN), 90,
    91
Toxicity, 66–67
    acute, 68, 69–70
    chronic, 68, 70–72
Transference, 27, 28–29, 86, 130
Trials
    double–blind, 140–141, 143–150
    open–label, 117
    single–blind, 50–51, 52–58,
        63–64, 110–111, 113–114, 118,
        136–137
Tricyclics, 21
Tryptophan, 63
Tuberculosis, 11
Typical depression. See Melancholic
    depression.
Tyramine, 12

U.S. Environmental Protection
    Agency (EPA), 70

Vanadium, 50
Vitamin C, 50, 52–53

Wallace, Mike, 20
Weight, 8–9, 95, 159, 174, 175
West, E. D., 10
Willis, Thomas, 101
Winokur, Andrew, 104
Winter blues. See Seasonal affective
    disorder (SAD).
Womack, Nathan, 42–43
World Health Organization, 69

Zoloft, 32–33, 44, 45, 51, 52, 53, 57,
    58, 59, 63, 110, 111, 113, 117